Free INDEED

AFRICAN-AMERICAN CHRISTIANS AND THE STRUGGLE FOR EQUALITY

CALLIE SMITH GRANT

BARBOUR
PUBLISHING

CONTENTS

Introduction 5

James W. C. Pennington 15

Harriet Tubman 61

Mary McLeod Bethune 113

Rosa Parks 161

INTRODUCTION

The four people whose stories are told in this book represent a span of two centuries of African-Americans, ranging from before the Civil War up to the present. Two of these four people were born into slavery but managed to get to free land and go on to make their marks in the nineteenth century. The other two did their work in the twentieth century. Each gained his or her particular kind of freedom at great personal risk, and each deeply believed God was on his or her side. Indeed, their efforts seemed to be blessed, and they dedicated their lives to helping others achieve much of what they had achieved.

James W. C. Pennington walked away from the plantation, his family, and all he knew. He went on to learn to read, to become an evangelist, and to write a stunning book about his experiences.

Harriet Tubman escaped slavery via the Underground Railroad. She became known as "Moses" because of her unfailing work at bringing hundreds more out of slavery.

Mary McLeod Bethune saw illiteracy as a unique kind of bondage, and she worked tirelessly throughout her life to bring education and other advantages to African-Americans.

And one simple act of civil disobedience by Rosa Parks, the "Mother of the Civil Rights Movement," sparked an event that would net astounding results in black America's fight for freedom.

The United States of America has been a melting pot of races and nationalities since its beginning. We take pride in that fact as Americans, even though we still have far to go to live together as peacefully as we should. But the blending of different people in our nation has not happened without great difficulty.

A specific stain in American history is that our nation was built—both before and after the American Revolution—on the backs of black people. Kidnapped out of their villages in Africa, these people were thrown into the holds of ships and transported across the Atlantic under the most horrible conditions. Should they make it through this long journey to America alive—and a certain percentage always perished at sea—they then became slaves for the rest of their lives, to be bought and sold like cattle.

Slavery in the United States was sanctioned by the British, used by the colonists, and continued by the new American patriots for the better part of a century following independence, particularly in the southern states. The buying and selling of human beings had a disastrous effect upon the morality of America, and our nation is still working its way through this colossal mistake.

Why did the new Americans—people who insisted on their own personal freedom from the British and who started a heroic revolution to get such freedom—own slaves in the first place? The simple answer seems to be greed.

Despite the cruelty inherent in owning human beings and in keeping them in an almost constant state of deprivation and fear, slave owners needed the cheap labor of slaves to build and work plantations and to sustain the good life.

In addition, in times when crops weren't doing so well or profits weren't as high from them, slaves became something to fall back on economically, a product of the plantation that owners would sell for profit, often splitting up families in the process. Since slaves worked hard under threat of bodily harm and were not paid anything at all, the labor couldn't be any cheaper. This is why plantations were so lavish.

Certainly some slave owners—many of whom professed to be believers in Christ—knew slavery was wrong, but only a very few felt convicted to free their slaves before the law forced them to do so. And certainly some slave owners were kinder than others, but the evidence is glaring that even they would break up families and sell individuals when the plantation needed cash. The fact is that most slave owners chose to believe that slaves were not actually humans, that they were something between animal and human, and that they simply did not have souls. This kind of thinking helped slave owners feel justified in their inhumane treatment of fellow human beings.

England came to her senses and voluntarily abandoned slavery in the early 1800s. But America did not, despite many voices crying out against it. Slaves certainly knew the institution of slavery was wrong in the eyes of God. So did abolitionists—Quakers, Methodists, and former slaves who managed to escape bondage. These people were very vocal and active at great personal risk to get slavery abolished in the United States. Until that happened, they were instrumental in illegally moving thousands of slaves to freedom via the Underground Railroad.

It took the long and bloody Civil War with its thousands of casualties to get slavery abolished in the United States. Yet even after the Emancipation Proclamation set slaves free, the conditions of African-Americans in the United States remained appalling. Though the lives of African-Americans who lived in the South were particularly trying, most black citizens all over the nation lived in poverty and inferior conditions. Throughout almost a century following emancipation, most blacks remained illiterate because education was not considered a priority. Black Americans were even afraid to exercise their right to vote in many states.

In addition, the Ku Klux Klan was born, wreaking havoc on blacks in both the North and the South. The law chose to ignore the terrorizing antics of the Klan, leaving black people helpless to protect themselves. The law even turned a blind eye toward lynching—the public hangings of black men by Klansmen and other white mobs. And lynching happened too often.

After decades spent living supposedly as free citizens but in reality still subject to the rule and the frequent violence of whites, it was black Americans themselves who initiated changes and fought for their freedom. They began working as a community to gain true equality through the legal system. When working through the legal system failed to create meaningful change, as was often the case, African-Americans used civil disobedience in what is known as the Civil Rights Movement. They worked together for decades, considering their fight sanctioned by God. And most amazingly, they did their part peacefully and dedicated to the absence of hate.

Civil disobedience is a time-honored tradition in the United States. It means that when the law of the land interferes with the laws of God or even the rules of basic decency, the people feel no responsibility to obey the law of the land. They express this through organized protest, boycotts, or more direct refusals, such as the Boston Tea Party, when colonists destroyed boatloads of tea for which they had been highly taxed without any government representation.

Black Americans knew that freedom and basic rights as human beings were God-given and that no other human being should tamper with that. They knew they were made in the image of God, and that to do God's work, they needed to be free. James W. C. Pennington phrased it clearly in a letter to his former master when he wrote: "The nature which God gave me did not allow me to believe that you had any more right to [own] me than I had to [own] you, and that was just none at all."

To facilitate their quest for freedom, black citizens formed organizations. These organizations, born mostly at the beginning of the twentieth century, usually had to meet in secret, especially in the South. Black Americans had a long history of meeting in secret, beginning in the days of slavery when plantation owners felt threatened by any gathering of slaves other than for supervised work. Even gathering for church was suspect. Slaves simply learned how to work around this, meeting for worship in groves of trees which deadened sound and communicating to one another in creative ways—particularly through song—even in the presence of unsuspecting whites.

After the Civil War, many Southern whites continued to be suspicious of gatherings of blacks. The church itself became the only legal meeting place for black Southerners, and this was where congregants learned information that would never make the newspapers. Pastors of those churches became leaders, the most famous being

Dr. Martin Luther King Jr.

Most black people in the North American colonies and in the early days of the United States had become believing Christians. During the era of slavery, Africans came to this country with their own native religions, but the practices of those religions were banned by white owners. At some point, most slaves in the early days seem to have converted to Christianity because of its compelling call to those in bondage; and as subsequent generations of black Americans were born, Christianity spread among the black American population.

The Bible speaks of bondage often. The stand taken by the children of Israel against Pharaoh modeled for African-Americans God's support in their longing for freedom and, later on, in their fight for basic rights and dignity. Generations of African-Americans would adopt as a rallying cry the demand "Let my people go!"

Hymns and spirituals took on double meaning. Every slave and civil rights worker knew the day would come when pain and trials would be over, and that would be the day they died and went to be with their Maker. In the meantime, however, the situation could, should, and would someday improve here on earth; God supported it. That was the second meaning to these spirituals. Two favorite spirituals in both slavery days and during the Civil Rights Movement were:

> *O freedom*
> *O freedom*
> *O freedom over me*
> *And before I'd be a slave*
> *I'd be buried in my grave*
> *And go home to my Lord and be free*

And:

> *I am bound for the freedom land,*
> *I am bound for the freedom land,*
> *O who will come and go with me?*
> *I am bound for the freedom land.*

Sometimes the lyrics of those spirituals were codes for slaves, acknowledging in song that someone was available to take them north and when it would happen. Often this information came in songs about the land of Canaan, which was a specific code for Canada, the country that was not only north but absolutely free territory for a slave. Harriet Tubman was known to wear disguises and walk through slave quarters at night singing such songs, both as praise to God and as a message to tell those slaves who wished to escape that the time was at hand.

Ironically, even a white Englishman, the former slave-runner John Newton, would express the double blessings of his conversion to Christ and his moral decision to turn away from buying and selling human beings when he wrote what is today the most popular hymn in America:

> *Amazing grace, how sweet the sound*
> *that saved a wretch like me;*
> *I once was lost but now am found,*
> *was blind, but now I see.*

It was a song that the Civil Rights Movement itself would one day embrace.

The African-American fight for freedom with its accompanying determination to treat others as Christ would treat them—peacefully, with dignity, and without hate—was unfortunately a long and often violent one. But history shows that it has been successful, and even though racial relations in America still have a long way to go, African-Americans have accomplished much in the history of our nation: the right to be a free individual in the world; the right to expect protection by the law; the right to public education; the right to vote; the right to assemble; the right to travel on public transportation or shop in stores with dignity and respect; the right to receive pay equal to that of whites. The list goes on and on.

Sadly, an area that still needs work is the segregated quality of most churches in America and even their denominations. In the 1990s, however, dialogue finally began between black churches who supported and worked in the Civil Rights Movement and white churches who chose to ignore the horrific conditions endured by their black brothers and sisters in Christ. The dialogues continue.

In the meantime, we can take inspiration from the lives of believing African-Americans in our nation's history, four of whose stories are told in the following pages. Every one of their lives was begun in poverty and with the prospect of danger lurking about at all times. Every one of these individuals moved beyond such difficult beginnings with a goal in mind and a faith to sustain him or her. And they all gave God praise for the successes they achieved.

James W. C. Pennington wanted freedom, an education, and the opportunity to evangelize. He achieved those goals, and he went on to write and publish a book about them. He even evangelized to his former master.

Harriet Tubman wanted freedom. Then she wanted it for her family. Then she wanted it for as many people as she could manage to steer in freedom's direction. She accomplished those goals, miraculously never losing a "passenger" on her dangerous journeys north.

Mary McLeod Bethune wanted an education. Then she made certain education was available to other impoverished black people, both children and adults. She went on to become the friend and confidante of an American president and his first lady, by which she helped bring more advantages to black American citizens. She accomplished many goals.

Rosa Parks wanted not only basic rights as a citizen but the dignity that should accompany those rights. She sparked a specific fight for that dignity, and she continued her work for the black community into old age. She, too, accomplished many goals.

These individuals seem almost mythic when we read about them and their amazing achievements. Indeed, spending time in any library's section on African-Americans and learning about the many black heroes of our nation is a thrilling experience.

At the same time, it's important to remember that the individuals in this book were flesh and blood, not perfect, not without faults. We can take heart that mere human beings—with God's love and blessing—accomplished so much in their time on earth. We can hope to do as much ourselves.

James W. C.
PENNINGTON

ONE

He didn't carefully plan it. One day, he'd had enough. One day the last indignity took place. One day he was certain his life was in immediate jeopardy if he stayed. One day he knew the time was right, and he walked off the plantation. Then he ran. At age twenty, a young blacksmith slave named Jim Pembroke—later to be known as James W. C. Pennington—began a harrowing journey to freedom.

It was a damp, chilly day in the marshes of Maryland in January 1807 when Nelly Pembroke, wife of fellow slave Bazil Pembroke, gave birth to her second child, a boy. Baby James yelled strong and loud as he made his entrance into the world. His mother could hear that he was healthy, and she thanked God for that as she watched the midwife clean up the little newborn. Nelly took her wide-eyed baby and held him close to feed him.

Gazing down at little James, Nelly thought she already

could see dignified features in his baby face. His dark, wide-set eyes searched around in the dim cabin's light in the way of newborns, focusing on everything and nothing, and a tiny scowl appeared on his forehead. She thought of the baby's granddaddy, the man who she'd always been told had been a Mandingo prince back in Africa. Kidnapped by slavers, he had been brought to the American colonies around 1746 and made a slave in Maryland. Now the prince had yet another descendant, and Nelly had a still-shining hope that this child might not be a slave forever. That was cause for celebration. Nelly rocked her boy in her arms and prayed that he would grow up a strong, healthy, and—one day—free man.

While certainly there was celebration in the slave quarters over baby James's birth, there was also cause for more worry than usual that same year. A short time after James's birth, the plantation's master, James Tilghman, died. His heir was to take over, and this was the worrisome part. A slave's future was precarious at best while the master of the plantation lived. Once the plantation passed down to other hands, invariably some if not all the slaves were sold. And when that happened, families—even families with newborn babies—were split up, usually forever.

In the days of American slavery, Maryland was one of the smallest slaveholding states. The great Chesapeake Bay divides Maryland down the middle, and what are called the "eastern shore" and the "western shore" are on either side of the Bay. Baby James was born and raised on the eastern shore.

Maryland made its living off crops such as wheat, rye, field corn (then called Indian corn), and tobacco. With slavery providing so much free manpower and that manpower producing an abundance of harvest year after year, the physical land eventually became exhausted for consistent growth of good crops. This was especially true where tobacco was grown, a crop that, in particular, depletes nutrients from soil. When soil got tired, many slaveholders, who had no intention of giving up their wealth or their high style of living, began raising, buying, and selling slaves as their main source of income, much as they would livestock.

Most of these slaveholders would sell their slaves when they deemed it necessary to other plantations in the Deep South where labor was still greatly needed. This was accomplished by selling slaves to a third party—the dreaded chain gang, a traveling group of slaves owned by an agent and transported south on foot. The chain gang would come through an area and deals were made, sometimes on the master's whim that day. Then individual slaves found themselves sold, literally chained to other unfortunate human beings, and walked the many states south. Even kind masters who found themselves in financial straits chose their fortunes over whatever compassion they may have had for the slaves on their land, and these masters bought and sold those human beings as briskly as anyone else did, thereby breaking up families and subjecting black people to a most humiliating existence over which they had no control.

Unfortunately, the Pembroke family's fears of being separated were founded when within the first few years of baby James's life, the master's son, Frisby Tilghman, took James, his older brother, and his mother to another farm near Hagerstown in Washington County, two hundred miles away, thereby breaking up the family. Nelly and Bazil Pembroke were owned by different slaveholders, and the laws of American slavery dictated that the children go with the mother. In those days of slow transportation and little leisure time, even living on adjacent farms would mean separated family members would see one another only on Sundays, if they were lucky to have that time off. To have a separation of many more miles meant family members might see each other only once a year on Christmas. And if a slave was sold to the South, that slave was split from his or her family essentially forever.

Fortunately, the Pembroke family separation was not to last long, as Frisby Tilghman saw the value of buying James's father, and the family was intact once again. For this they were grateful, but they knew better than to breathe easy. Tilghman had broken them up before; if he felt he needed to, he would certainly do it again.

James, his older brother, Robert, and eventually ten more siblings grew up on the Tilghman plantation. James was loved by his family very much, but his childhood was not a happy one. First of all, his parents were too busy working to parent him during the day. Left to his own devices, he was often hungry. He played with other slave children until he was old enough to contribute work to the farm, but this was not a secure environment for a child. He was subject to being swatted around by the plantation overseers for their personal enjoyment, and he was allowed to see the horrible ways in which adult slaves—even his own parents—were treated at the hands of the white men in charge. Through these dark years of childhood, something was born in James's heart at an early age—a burning dignity that needed freedom.

At the tender age of nine, James and his brother Robert were sent to town about six miles away to work for another family. Often slaveholders would "hire out" slaves to non-slaveholders for money and so young slaves could learn a useful trade. James was taught the work of stonemasonry, and life was marginally better at this time because he was away from the cruelties of his particular master and living with people who did not own him or any other slaves. And though little James was away from his parents, Robert—the brother to whom James was most attached—was nearby.

This lasted for two years. James returned home with a trade, but Robert stayed away and eventually was bought by someone in the area. Their separation was permanent at this point, devastating young James.

Back home, at age eleven, James was put in the apprenticeship of the plantation blacksmith, and this became James's trade, an occupation from which he took pleasure and pride in his work and craftsmanship. Besides shoeing horses, this young blacksmith made hammers, hatchets, knives, and even pistols.

Eventually James was sold to another plantation for seven hundred dollars. That plantation found that it did not have sufficient work to keep James busy enough to earn his keep, so he was for sale again. Tilghman bought him back.

James's distress from having no control over his personal circumstances grew more and more inside him. At any point, Tilghman could decide any aspect of James's fate or that of any member of his family. It was a realization fraught with anxiety.

Six months after returning to Tilghman's plantation, at the age of twenty, James, as he would express it many years later, "determined to fly."

TWO

Frisby Tilghman was in a foul mood that Monday morning, and everyone knew it. Two slaves—one of them James's uncle—had not made it back in time from their Sunday visits to other plantations, and Tilghman vowed he would make them pay for it. It soon became clear that every other slave would pay who came in Tilghman's path that morning.

One of the unlucky ones was James's father. Bazil Pembroke was in charge of the plantation's valuable Merino sheep, and that morning he was feeding a lamb by hand when Tilghman began complaining to him about the slaves who had not yet come in. In the course of his tirade, Tilghman barked to Bazil, "The fact is, I have too many of you. My people are getting to be the most careless, lazy, and worthless in the county."

Bazil continued to feed the lamb, but he felt compelled to say, "Master, I am always at my post. Monday morning never finds me off the plantation."

"Hush, Bazil," Tilghman snapped back. "I shall have to sell some of you, and then the rest will have enough to do. I do not have enough work to keep you all employed. I have too many of you."

At this point, Bazil Pembroke, feeling personally insulted, gently said, "If I am one of too many, sir, give me a chance to get a purchase, and I am willing to be sold when it may suit you."

This infuriated Tilghman. He took a whip and beat Bazil with fifteen or twenty lashes across his back. James had been getting his breakfast nearby and heard the entire exchange. He was then forced to listen to each lash that was put on his own father, powerless to stop it. Later he would relay how particularly horrible it was to know that his father was attacked while he was in the process of the most gentle of farmwork, the feeding of a baby lamb. Tilghman felt free to beat Bazil as if he were a beast.

The Pembrokes were horrified at this treatment of their family patriarch. They whispered about it at night in the slave quarters for the next week. James found that he could no longer take pleasure in the craftsmanship of his blacksmith work as he had before, and it became clear to him that Tilghman sensed his displeasure and was watching him carefully.

His fears were confirmed one day when he was kneeling down shoeing a horse, not realizing Tilghman was watching him. James stood to straighten his back, glanced around him, and accidentally made eye contact with Tilghman.

Eye contact was always avoided between black and white in the slaveholding South, a custom which would take another century past the end of slavery to correct. There were strict rules of body language between master and slave, for one thing, and those rules dictated that slaves keep their eyes lowered or averted. But there was also a collective fear among white slaveholders that slaves would one day rise up and kill their masters. The fear about this was great. So in spite of their bullying, white masters were actually afraid of black men. And eye contact was viewed as a challenge.

Such was the case on this day. "What are you rolling your eyes at me for?" Tilghman shouted. Then he took his walking cane and beat James severely, swore at him, and walked off.

This numbered two beatings for the Pembroke family in a short time, both of them on older males. It was a significant development that worried them greatly, because it appeared that Tilghman was venting his anger on the Pembrokes personally. Thirteen of the plantation's thirty-three slaves were Pembrokes, and the family was gravely concerned that they were in jeopardy of being punished further by being split up and sold—or at the very least, subject to more beatings whenever Tilghman flew into a rage.

Then they learned that Tilghman had a house servant watching the family and reporting on their every move. Nelly spoke to the servant, attempting to shame him for his betrayal. The man in turn went to Tilghman, who called in James, Bazil, and Nelly together and accused them of plotting against him. When Nelly told Tilghman that she had been the only one to speak to the spying servant, Tilghman threatened Nelly with a severe beating if she ever spoke to the man again. And of course the threat of selling and splitting up the family continued to loom large.

James's heart broke listening to this. A few days later, he wrapped up a bundle of clothes, hid them in a cave at the outskirts of the farm, and made plans without telling a soul. He was tortured with the decision whether or not to tell his parents and his four brothers and six sisters who lived on the plantation that he planned to leave. Of course he wanted to say his good-byes to his beloved family whom in all probability he might never see again. But he knew they would be interrogated and threatened when his absence was discovered. For that reason, he decided it would be best not to let them know anything about his plans so that their surprise and shock at his missing would be obvious and genuine.

His other worry was that, though he was determined to leave, he had no idea how to get where he needed to go or how to go about finding help. He'd rarely been away from home, so his knowledge of geography was tightly local. He knew Pennsylvania was a free state, and he knew Philadelphia would be a good destination in that state. He knew it was north, but how far north? He knew he should follow the North Star—every slave had that fact imbedded in their memory should they one day need to use it—but where was Pennsylvania in relation to Maryland? How would he know it when he saw it?

And how could he do this without help? Slavery in 1828 was not yet the hotbed moral issue it would become in later years, so the Underground Railroad—an illegal system of moving slaves to freedom—was not as prevalent. James knew he had a completely foreign journey ahead of him, entirely on foot and highly vulnerable, and he was truly at the mercy of God.

Another thing that magnified James's worry was that in his recollection, no other slave had escaped this plantation. He knew of escapees from other plantations who were dragged back, beaten severely, then sold south, never to be seen or heard from again. He knew this could very well become his fate, too. The risk was huge.

But there was something inside James that told him he needed to leave now. As he would later write: "How the impression came to be upon my mind I cannot tell; but there was a strange and horrifying belief that if I did not set the crisis that day, I should be self-doomed. The hour was come, and the man must act or forever be a slave."

That hour was two o'clock in the afternoon on Sunday, October 28, 1828.

THREE

James walked as nonchalantly as he could through the slave quarter that Sunday afternoon, looking around for the last time at all that was familiar. Sundays were a day of rest for most slaves, so there wasn't a lot of hustle and bustle, just some children playing. Adults were visiting with each other quietly or napping.

He looked for food for his journey as casually as he could, but he only came upon some corn bread, and he stuffed his pockets with about a half pound of it. Then he moved on through the barnyard and beyond. He reached the cave at the edge of the farm where he had left his bundle of clothes the day before, grabbed the bundle, and headed for the cover of the thick woods. In a matter of minutes, he was on his way, and now there could be no turning back.

James's first destination would be the town six miles away where his brother Robert lived. James desperately wanted to inform at least this sibling—his most revered one—of his plans and even seek his advice. But in the end,

James chose not to contact Robert, thereby sparing him any more trouble than necessary.

His heart aching, James moved on past Robert's town under the cover of darkness. He kept moving quickly, his good sense telling him that whether or not he knew where he was going, he must put as much distance between himself and the plantation as possible before Monday morning. As he would later write, "I therefore set forth in sorrowful earnest, only now and then I was cheered by the wild hope that I should somewhere and at sometime be free."

That first night was a rough one for James, both physically and mentally. He knew he would only be safe if he moved at night and hid by day, and that first night he was able to cover a lot of ground due to good weather and probably adrenaline. But by three o'clock in the morning, he was chilled from the dew and very discouraged. It was a frightening predicament to be in since going on loomed more and more terrifying, but going back was not an option.

As daylight broke, James found himself in an open field, and he scurried to find a place to hide for the day. The only shelter he could find was a large cornstalk a few hundred yards from the road, under which he took cover. There he was forced to pass the day in a squatting position, hungry and anxious.

It would be hard to imagine squatting all day with nothing to do but worry. But that's what James did. By nightfall, his state of anxiety was even higher than it had been the day before, and he was faced with moving on without rest and, by now, without food. As if all that weren't enough, the sky was so cloudy that the North Star was not visible. Nevertheless, as darkness blanketed the area, James moved out from under the cornstalk and headed in the direction he hoped was north.

By morning he came upon fresh water and some sour apples, which he devoured. He found a small bridge in the road, tucked into its arch, and was able to hide well enough to get some rest, though his stomach was cramped from the bad food and worry. That night he moved on in the dark, stopping to doze every now and then.

At dawn of the third day, he came upon a rather public road and saw a white child about twelve years old. He took the risk to ask the boy where the road led to and was told that it would end up in Baltimore, about eighteen miles away. James had always heard that Baltimore was eighty miles from the plantation. This meant he had traveled over sixty miles from home at this point, but obviously he was still in Maryland, which was not good. He asked the boy which was the best way to Philadelphia and was told that he could reach it through Baltimore. So he headed down the road, watching and listening for any other traffic.

He came upon another young white man with a load of hay who asked him where he was going. James told him Philadelphia. The young man had a kind way about him, and he asked James if he was a free man. James said he was. The young man asked him if he had papers. Of course James knew that all free black men carried papers proving they were free which they showed whenever asked; otherwise the assumption would be that any black man on the road was on the run.

"No, sir," James said. "I have no papers."

"Well, my friend," said the young man, "you should not travel on this road. There are men living on this road who are constantly on the lookout for your people, and they will find you before you've gone three miles." He offered specific directions to a certain house where an old man would be willing to help James; then he went on his way.

This was confounding to James. He believed the white man wanted to help, but James was so fatigued and unsettled by his present danger and the fact that he was still in Maryland that he promptly forgot the young man's directions. He did leave the dangerous road and look for hiding, but it was too late. The morning had marched on, and people were up and about and at work in the fields. James kept walking, his mind buzzing.

By around ten o'clock in the morning, he came upon a tavern near the town of Reistertown. He moved past the tavern as rapidly as he could. A man digging potatoes by the road called to him in what James later described as a "coarse, stern voice."

"Who do you belong to?" the man called out.

"I am free, sir."

"Do you have papers?"

When James admitted he had no papers, the man rose from his work and came to him. "You'll have to stop here," he said.

James spoke as a free man. "My business is yonder, sir, and I do not wish to stop." He continued to walk briskly.

But the man hurried after him, exhorting him to stop.

James thought quickly. Should he run? Should he threaten to injure the man? Suddenly the man literally jumped on him and yelled for a neighbor to help. James managed to shake the man off and run.

As James took off, the first man gave chase. Then the second man joined in the pursuit with a knife in tow. They managed to grab hold of James, who desperately tried to figure out how to outsmart two men larger than he and armed. His heart sank when two more neighbor men joined the group. Now four men had him in tow, and they led him into the tavern.

What would they do with him?

FOUR

The day went from bad to worse for James as neighbors who had heard the ruckus joined the group in the tavern, everyone eager to see and talk about the mystery man they assumed to be a runaway. A great discussion ensued as to what to do with him. One man recommended jailing him until he confessed to whom he belonged. Another man tried cajoling the information out of James, promising not to jail him if he simply told them the truth. James continued to insist he was a free man.

During this morning, James had what he would later refer to as a "great moral dilemma," and it needed to be resolved in his mind so that he could move on and act consistently in this escape to freedom. The moral dilemma was this: When asked questions about his status as a slave, should he lie? Though James would later say that his response to the world at this time was not based on Scripture, these nevertheless were the days when a man's word was sometimes the most he had, and protecting that honest word mattered greatly. And James had been raised by moral parents who taught him "truth may be blamed but cannot be shamed."

On the other hand, James's very life was at stake. He later wrote about his thoughts that day: "The first point decided was the facts in this case are my private property. These men have no more right to them than a highway robber has to my purse. What will be the consequence if I put them in possession of the facts? In forty-eight hours, I shall have received forty-eight lashes and be on my way to the Louisiana cotton fields. . .[the captors] will get a paltry sum of two hundred dollars. Is not my liberty worth more to me than two hundred dollars are to them? I resolved therefore to insist that I was free."

He would go on to let the reader know that he had hated every minute of lying. He did not feel clever, as if he were pulling the wool over the eyes of stupid men; he simply felt compelled to save his very skin.

He reminded the reader that the institution of slavery was so evil that it begat more evil every step along the way, as evidenced in the stories he would make up on the early days of his frightening escape. He wrote: "Whatever my readers may think, therefore, of the history of events of the day, do not admire in it the fabrications; but see in it the impediments that often fall into the pathway of the flying bondman. See how human bloodhounds gratuitously chase, catch, and tempt him to shed blood and lie; how when he would do good, evil is thrust upon him."

So for the sake of his physical life—and because he truly felt he was a free man inside—James would continue to insist that he was not an escaped slave but rather a free man.

Nobody in the tavern believed him. The group decided they should tie James's hands and take him to a judge who would decide his fate. Two of the men began to lead James on foot to the judge's house about a half mile down the road, so beginning a series of events that at times might have been amusing had James's life not been in jeopardy.

First the judge was not home. The men were irritated but still resolved to perform what they considered their civic duty—to deal with this runaway slave. Together they moved on to another judge's house in the area. This required journeying through a field and over fences, and twenty minutes later, they reached the house of the second judge—who was not home.

By now it was early afternoon, and nobody was getting any work done, so busy were they with the runaway. They headed back the mile and a half to the tavern. This required more fence-climbing, which was difficult to maneuver with a bound man, so the two white men untied James for the journey. James moved strategically as soon as possible. In a stand of trees, he turned quickly and swept the legs out from under one of the men, knocking him to the ground. Then James ran for all his might.

Unfortunately, James Pembroke was a short man, about five feet five inches, and even though he was able to clear some fences and run through a field, a longer-legged man was gaining on him. Now James had another moral issue to consider: Should he injure his pursuer? If he could just get the right stone, he could attack him. But he had no chance for that, something for which he would later be grateful, as James was not by nature an aggressive individual. As he crested a hill, he saw that the field had recently been plowed up, which would slow down his progress—and then the farmer doing the plowing suddenly grabbed James by the collar.

Now everyone was unhappy. They threw James down and tied him up again, kicking him and cursing him. Then they dragged him back to the tavern, which they reached midafternoon, and there, as the men cooled off in the dark room with their neighbors, they strongly suggested James tell them who he was, where he was from, and who was his master.

By now James realized that his attempt at running had killed any chance of being believed that he was a free man. He also knew that it was a matter of a short time before concrete knowledge of his runaway status would reach the tavern in the form of fliers with a description of his appearance and a reward. After all, he was still in Maryland.

"If you will not put me in jail," James said, "I will tell you where I am from."

The men promised they would not jail him.

James went on, drawing on elements of every story he'd ever heard to come up with this one. "Well, a few weeks ago, I was sold to a slave trader who had a large chain gang. We set out for Georgia, but when we got to a town in Virginia, the slave trader was taken sick and died from smallpox. Several of the chain gang also died from it, so the people in the town became alarmed and did not want the gang to remain among them. No one claimed us or wished to have anything to do with us. I left the rest and thought I would go somewhere and get work."

This was a believable story, and the men in the tavern accepted it. In the nineteenth century, smallpox was a fairly common though lethal disease which some people survived and many did not. The fear of disease epidemics in these days before lifesaving medicines was so great that several men in the tavern immediately moved away from James, and some even hurried out, saying they should "let this smallpox slave go."

Those who stayed behind questioned James further,

and he made up a name for his master, a name the others claimed to recognize. They even asked him what kind of a man his master was, and James described the phantom man. One by one, the men in the tavern headed home. One was called by his wife, who complained bitterly that he'd lost an entire afternoon of work to this enterprise of chasing down a runaway, and she was not pleased.

The man who had originally apprehended James found himself left alone with him. He sighed. "I'm going to take you to the next town," he said, "and have you work for my brother until we can sort this all out. Will you agree to that?"

James did agree. He knew this development would present more opportunity to get away. Then the man suggested James eat. James sat down at four o'clock on Wednesday for his first real meal since Sunday morning. He put away as much food as he could, thinking how he would handle the next few hours. As he would later write, "Although I had so completely frustrated their designs for the moment, I knew that it would by no means answer for me to go into that town, where there were prisons, handbills, newspapers, and travelers.

"My intention was to start with him but not to enter the town alive."

FIVE

The meal was over, and it was time to set out on the journey. To James's surprise and relief, the white man and he would travel the four-mile trip on foot and not by wagon. That would give James time to think and advantage to move.

A mile or so down the road, they were joined by another white man. The two men spoke Dutch to each other, which James was not able to follow at first, but eventually he learned that this new man was one of the judges who had not been at his home that morning. Seated on his high horse and looking, as James would later describe, "not unlike a field marshal in the act of reviewing troops," the judge interrogated James, who slowly and carefully repeated his story, politely filling in details when asked.

The men decided James needed to stay in their vicinity until they could check out his story. They determined to go back to the tavern yet again, and there the judge continued to drill James on the details of his story. Finally satisfied, the judge offered to take James back to his own farm and pay him to work there for a while. James readily agreed to it, anticipating a chance to bolt, but when he realized he'd first have to spend the night at the farm of the first man, on a main Maryland road, he became worried.

As the judge rode away, James followed the first man back to his potato field, determined to run when the occasion presented itself. As instructed by the farmer, James worked for a few hours in the field with a team of horses under the watchful eye of the farmer's young son. James watched and waited for the right moment to bolt.

Finally the timing was perfect: James was able to get the team of horses riled up while the boy was off fetching water. James grabbed his chance and ran into the nearby woods, knowing correctly that the boy would have to get the team of horses under control before he could consider chasing James.

It worked. He spent the night in the woods moving, protected by a deep darkness. Barefoot, his clothes soaked through with sweat, he shivered uncontrollably, trying to keep his resolve intact. Again the night was overcast and the North Star not evident. Fear of animals, loss of direction, and the night chill took its toll on the frightened young man until dawn crawled up the eastern sky.

James came upon a small farm whose owners had not yet risen, and he decided to hide there for the day. In the barn, he eased himself into a corncrib using its fodder for cover. This was a pretty noisy endeavor, and a small house dog yapped furiously. Fortunately, nobody in the house paid any attention to its bark.

In the morning daylight, James watched the man of the house leave for the fields, and again, the rest of the family paid no attention to their rather vocal dog. James spent the day resting and smelling the tantalizing odors of cooking in the house. Everything in him wanted to approach the house's kitchen and ask the lady of the house for food, but he managed to keep himself from doing that.

It soon became obvious that it was a good thing he had refrained from leaving his corn fodder. In the midafternoon there was a lot of traffic on the road and a sense of agitation in the air. By listening carefully to wagons and horses going by, James discovered men were on the lookout for him. The locals now knew who he was. He heard one man read the unflattering way in which Tilghman described James on a posted flier: "very black, square and clumsily made, with a down look, prominent reddish eyes, and mumbles or talks with his teeth closed."

James listened to the men's speculations as to where in the woods he was hiding. Most disturbing were comments about how they would hang him on the spot when they found him. It took tremendous self-control for James to remain calm. He listened and trembled.

At dusk the man of the house returned to do chores in the barnyard. Again the dog was agitated, and again nobody paid attention. Then James heard the search party return and talk to the farmer. They talked about who James was, that he was a runaway blacksmith slave, and that there was a two-hundred-dollar reward out for his return, which was a great deal of money at the time.

The farmer promised to keep his eye open for James, and James was certain the barn was about to be searched. But after the search party left, the farmer went about his chores outdoors and never came near the barn. The dog continued to yap. The farmer continued to ignore the dog.

Nightfall came and James made his move. He ran through fields, marshes, and frost, and he used the road when he could. Exhausted, hungry, and chilled, he found another corn stack in a field, and there he crawled in, ate some field corn, and fell dead asleep, waking eventually to warm sunlight beating through his cover. Forced to stay in his corn stack throughout the day, he nibbled carefully on field corn and managed to take sustenance that way, enough so that when it was time to move on, he felt somewhat energized.

Now he made a new decision. He believed he was near free territory, so he resolved that he would at some point walk on the road and ask passersby for directions to Philadelphia. He moved to the main road and came to a tollgate. An older woman was there, a widow judging by her black garb, and she answered his questions kindly, clearly understanding without saying so the precarious circumstances the young black man before her was in.

Indeed he was in Pennsylvania, and the widow directed James three miles down the road to the house of William Wright, a Quaker farmer whom James would later refer to in his writings as W. W. She claimed the Quaker would be helpful, and James sensed that he could believe this woman.

After the three-mile trek in Adams County, Pennsylvania, James stood at the door of Wright's house and knocked. A kindly man opened the door, and James could see he was about to sit down to breakfast. James decided to approach the situation cautiously by asking the man for work.

Wright responded, "Well, come in and take thy breakfast and get warm, and we will talk about it. Thee must be cold without any coat."

This simple kindness was a defining moment in the journey of Jim Pembroke, fugitive slave. Here's what he would write about it later: "Come in and take thy breakfast and get warm. These words spoken by a stranger, but with such an air of simple sincerity and fatherly kindness, made an overwhelming impression upon my mind. They made me feel, spite of all my fear and timidity, that I had, in the providence of God, found a friend and a home. . . .

"From that day to this, whenever I discover the least disposition in my heart to disregard the wretched condition of any poor or distressed persons with whom I meet, I call to mind these words—Come in, and take thy breakfast, and get warm."

The kind William Wright and his sweet wife kept James safe and hidden for the next six months. During this time, while James worked for them for his keep, the couple taught him to read and write in a method that was positive and kind. This was an amazing boon for an illiterate former slave.

And twenty-one-year-old James was beyond ready to learn to read and write. Even so, he could hardly have imagined that one day he would be an eloquent speaker and writer and the author of a best-selling book that would still be read well over a century later.

SIX

As William Wright and his wife taught James to read and write, James realized what had been missing in his life. Part of it was educational, but part of it was spiritual. He had never read a Bible, and in fact he knew only a few stories from it that had been told in the slave quarters back home. He realized yet another evil of slavery in keeping human beings from a faith in God and knowledge of Christ and His teachings. And there was no substitute for reading the Bible itself.

James also felt insecurities about the likelihood of getting anywhere in the world as a black man, even a free one. He would later write: "As my friend poured light into my mind, I saw the darkness; it amazed and grieved beyond description. Sometimes I sank down under the load and became discouraged and dared not hope that I could ever succeed in acquiring knowledge enough to make me happy or useful to my fellow beings.

"My dear friend W. W., however, had a happy tact to

inspire me with confidence, and he, perceiving my state of mind, exerted himself, not without success to encourage me. He cited to me various instances of colored persons of whom I had not heard before and who had distinguished themselves for learning. . . ." One such shining example was the black poet Phyllis Wheatley, whose poems James came to love.

It was a new world for the blacksmith, a new kind of apprenticeship. He grew in knowledge and in spirit. He would later wish his six months at the Wright home could have been six years. But the possibility of capture continued to be a real one. For both his sake and the sake of his kind benefactors, when March came, James moved on toward Philadelphia as he had originally planned. Again, it was good timing; within a month or two, James's former master was seen twenty miles away from the Wright home still in an active search for James.

En route to Philadelphia, James found himself again the recipient of the kind mercies of Quakers. This sect of Christians believed in the sanctity of life so greatly that they quietly defied laws of the land to help runaway slaves become free and start a new life. The civil disobedience of the Quakers of the nineteenth century would greatly contribute to the success of the Underground Railroad.

James lived for a while in Chester County, Pennsylvania, on a farm owned by a Quaker couple, whom he referred to as Mr. and Mrs. K. Again he worked for his keep. Mrs. K. gave him his first Bible to own, a tremendous thrill for the new student and new believer. At every opportunity, James read the Bible voraciously and memorized passages. While doing farmwork, he began making up and speaking sermons as if he had an audience, working out scriptural issues aloud. There in the fields, a former slave was being groomed for the call to preach.

After seven months with the kind Quakers, James knew it was once again time to move on, this time because he yearned for more education. The K family sent him off with letters of recommendation. James passed through Philadelphia and on to New York, where, with the threat of slavers showing up to claim him even there, he decided to settle down and start his life rather than move on to Canada. He later noted, "I often felt serious apprehensions of danger, and yet I felt also that I must begin in the world somewhere."

Sometime during these years, James changed his name, both for safety and for a sense of identity. The slave Jim Pembroke became James W. C. Pennington.

In New York James settled in Brooklyn, where he worked as a coachman for decent wages. At the same time, he attended night school and paid for private tuition, as well. It was a fruitful time for James.

But all was not rosy inside the young man during these early years of life in the North. Though he relished his new-found freedom greatly, more and more he felt keenly the disadvantage of his late start in education. He would often be quoted later from his writings as saying: "There is one sin that slavery committed against me, which I never can forgive. It robbed me of my education; the injury is irreparable; I feel the embarrassment more seriously now than I ever did before. It cost me two years' hard labor, after I fled, to unshackle my mind; it was three years before I had purged my language of slavery's idioms; it was four years before I had thrown off the crouching aspect of slavery; and now the evil that besets me is a great lack of that general information, the foundation of which is most effectually laid in that part of life which I served as a slave." He ended the essay with: "I shall have to go to my last account with this charge against the system of slaver: Vile monster! Thou has hindered my usefulness by robbing me of my early education!"

These early years of living as a free man in New York were also ones of tremendous spiritual growth for young James. In the spring of 1829, he felt an increasing burden for the victims of slavery—both the slaves, whom he hoped "may be speedily released from the pain of drinking a cup whose bitterness I have sufficiently tasted," and also the masters whose complicity in an evil institution must truly be dangerous to their souls. He wrote, "The only harm I wish to slaveholders is that they may be speedily delivered from the guilt of a sin, which, if not repented of, must bring down the judgment of Almighty God upon their devoted heads."

He began a system of prayer and fasting over slavery. Spiritually, this was new territory to James, but he felt led to do it. He sought counsel from more grounded believers and was encouraged to work through his issues of faith, with the full belief that God was watching him and available to him.

During the weeks of meditation, the clear question came to James's heart: What shall I do for the slave? In these days, the many antislavery organizations that would eventually exist in America were not yet born. James would seem to be on his own if he intended to be an advocate for freeing slaves.

But he found he was not alone at all, and he began meeting many freed slaves in New York. He joined the American Colonization Society, whose members—new missionaries of sorts—began gathering and holding conventions to determine what they as African-Americans could do to stop the soul-damaging institution of slavery.

Another change was brewing in James, and the young man who preached to the barnyard felt a call to offer his services to slaves in some meaningful way. To that end, he studied for the ministry in the Presbyterian denomination.

In the meantime, in 1834, James was approached by an associate to teach school in Brooklyn. The eager student who had himself only recently learned to read was asked to teach others. He agreed to it and was given a salary of two hundred dollars per year—the same sum offered for his capture not so long ago.

It was five years, three months, and thirteen days after James had arrived from the South.

SEVEN

James Pennington taught school for five years, during which he studied for the ministry. He was ordained as a Presbyterian minister in 1837, and he took an assistant pastorate in the Presbyterian church in Brooklyn. He went on to become the pastor of two African-American Congregational churches in New York.

A woodcut portrait of James made during this prime of his life shows a handsome, clean-shaven man, slightly scowling, wearing the minister's garb of the day—a starched white scarf crossed neatly at the throat atop a dark clerical robe. Heavy eyebrows meet and cross over the bridge of his nose. His large, wide-set eyes seem somber and mildly sad as they gaze off to the side of the artist.

James married a woman named Harriet who also was devoted to the cause of freedom. During these years, helping to free individuals from slavery was one of this couple's major undertakings. But making education available to African-Americans was also a constant goal in James and Harriet's life together. They became active in the New York Society for the Promotion of Education among Colored Children.

In 1841, as part of his teaching mission, James wrote and published one of the earliest histories of black people in existence, titled *A Text Book of the Origin and History of the Colored People.* Though the book was intended to be a textbook for his young students, it was actually too advanced for that. Nevertheless, its content was certainly impressive. It also kicked off a side career as a professional writer for the man who had been silenced for too many years.

In 1843 James was named a delegate to the Connecticut State Anti-Slavery Society for its world convention. Simultaneously, he was asked to represent the American Peace Society at their world convention. Both conventions were held in London that year, and Pennington had the golden opportunity of officially addressing the antislavery convention in a speech that attracted much attention. He continued to speak extensively throughout Great Britain, and so began a love between James and that country which would pay off greatly in the future.

As James became a more public and prominent speaker and advocate for abolishing slavery, his whereabouts became public knowledge. In 1844 an antislavery newsletter inadvertently gave away his address. Although this period predates the Fugitive Slave Act of 1850, in which the nation agreed to let Southern slaveholders come north and capture their runaways, it was a worrisome thing to have his address made public. This famous, educated man of the cloth could still actually be captured and taken back into slavery. The only recourse to not looking over his shoulder for the rest of his life was to attempt to gain his freedom legally. He set about putting those wheels in motion in 1846.

That same year, Harriet died, and James felt increased

longing to be with his family, the Pembrokes. He determined that he would contact his former master, Frisby Tilghman, and negotiate to purchase not only himself, something slaves could sometimes do, but at the same time, he would seek to purchase his parents.

Tilghman had sold and bought back Nelly and Bazil Pembroke during years of unfortunate circumstances on the plantation that were leading to financial failure, and he had also sold off all ten of James's brothers and sisters. The intricacies of state slave laws at the time dictated that James's aging parents should have been freed by now, but a loophole entitled Tilghman to officially declare Nelly and Bazil Pembroke "slaves for life." He even had paperwork to that effect.

James's strategy was to offer to send money to Tilghman for both his parents and for himself through a third party, a man named John Hooker. James gathered together all the funds he could by saving his wages, selling his library of beloved books, and getting funds from concerned citizens. He poured everything into this endeavor.

Hooker contacted Tilghman, who consented to let James purchase himself but said nothing about the whereabouts of the elder Pembrokes. It turned out he did not own them anymore, though he never admitted that. In addition, Tilghman greatly offended James when he wrote to John Hooker: "The ungrateful servant in whose behalf you write merits no clemency from me. He was guilty of theft when he departed, for which I hope he has made due amends. . . . Servants are selling from $550 to $700. I will take $550 and liberate him." He added a postscript: "Jim was a first-rate mechanic [blacksmith] and was worth to me $1,000."

James had not seen his parents in so many years, and he was mortified both by Tilghman's refusal to deal with him on behalf of the old folks and also by the false accusation of theft. At this point, James himself wrote to Tilghman stating that he would never enter into an agreement with the former master that did not include James's parents. Then he went about seeking their freedom in other ways. Eventually most of James's family members made it to Canada via the Underground Railroad or were freed by other methods—marrying into freedom or gaining free papers from masters. James himself eventually paid $150 to Tilghman's estate for his own freedom.

During these years, James was known as a leader in the cause of the abolition of slavery both in the northern United States and in England. Nevertheless, it was a tremendous surprise to him when, in 1849, the London publishing house of Charles Gilpin offered to publish James's story of escaping slavery.

James wrote the subsequent slave narrative himself and referred to it as a "tract," which was a booklet of sorts intended to persuade the reader in some direction, usually salvation or abstinence from alcohol. In this case it was the cause of the abolition of slavery. The book was titled and subtitled: *The Fugitive Blacksmith, or Events in the History of James W. C. Pennington, Pastor of a Presbyterian Church, New York.*

James's slim book was a page-turner. It included his account of his life as a slave and his thrilling escape from slavery only twenty years before, as well as pertinent letters and essays on the subjects of slavery and personal salvation. *The Fugitive Blacksmith* became the talk of the English readership and soon was such a raving success that it sold out its first print run in record time. It sold out its second print run just as quickly. The publisher hurried back to press for a third printing within a year, the same year the United States put into effect its shameful Fugitive Slave Act.

British readers were captivated by Pennington's eloquent yet straightforward style of storytelling, his clear reasoning behind the need to stop the horrors of slavery, and his passionate plea for readers to help him bring more slaves out of bondage.

The British press loved the book. *Christian Witness* called it an "entrancing narrative." *Nonconformist* said: "The principal portion of the 'Tract,' as Mr. Pennington modestly styles his book, consists of an autobiography of his early life as a slave and of his escape from bondage and final settlement in New York as a Presbyterian minister. His adventures and hair-breadth escapes invest the narrative with startling interest and excite the deepest sympathies of the reader."

James's concern over fellow slaves in America touched a nerve with the British, who had only recently voluntarily stopped the buying and selling of human beings in their own country and in their colonies throughout the world. They fully stood behind this former slave whose writing showed such a profound and surprising command of their mother tongue—and whose storytelling left them almost breathless. They encouraged one another to purchase copies of the book so that James could use that money to fund the escapes of more fugitive slaves, which he did. *Christian Witness* said: "We very cordially recommend him and his narrative to the kind consideration of our readers. Let them load him with English hospitality, fill his purse, and send him back as fast as possible to the land of his early bondage, of his matured freedom, and to the people to whose character and capabilities he does so much honor."

The Fugitive Blacksmith not only told James's compelling autobiography, it also gave him a chance to talk about the institution of slavery. James's style was not to personally slam his former master, but to show the evil that came from the institution of slavery itself; therefore, anyone involved in such a horrible thing was bound to commit evil acts. One of his more compelling topics in both orating and writing had to do with the myth of the "kind" master about which James offered unique insights. While he allowed that certainly men differed and some were kinder than others, even "kind" masters abused slaves, split up families, and sold human beings to others less kind. Such were the unavoidable results of the institution of slavery.

Another unavoidable result of slavery James wrote about was how slaveholders' families deteriorated over time. James wrote, "There is no one feature of slavery to which the mind recurs with more gloomy impressions than to its disastrous influence upon the families of the masters. . . ." Slaves had always observed this phenomenon—that each generation of slaveholders in a family was more inferior than the one before, as if a family business of investing in slave labor simply could not survive morally or physically.

The pressures of keeping up a plantation with such a dismal and horrific way of financing itself—that is, the buying and selling and even breeding of human beings—indeed seemed to cause plantation success to deteriorate generation after generation and family members to show blatant lack of character in all ways. James suggested that the weakening of the plantation families was God's way of showing His displeasure and removing His blessing from such families.

The Fugitive Blacksmith gave James a platform to eloquently state his well-reasoned case in writing to thousands of readers, and it provided many speaking engagements throughout England and Europe for him to do the same. The British and Europeans adored James. He was even awarded an honorary doctorate of divinity from the

University of Heidelberg, the first African-American to receive such an honor.

There was one other important moment in James's life that was included in *The Fugitive Blacksmith*. He had felt moved to write a letter for many years, a letter which was subsequently printed in his book. By this point in his life, James was a master wordsmith who could eloquently state a case—whether it be in a speech about abolition or a sermon about salvation—and he was a published writer. Something had been on his mind for years now, something he needed to write about.

And he needed to write it directly to one specific reader—his former master, Frisby Tilghman.

EIGHT

In his letter to the man from whom he had escaped seventeen years before, James Pennington used all his reasoning skills, his talent at crafting ideas, and his gifts of persuasion to draft a long, straightforward letter. In it he laid open his heart while at the same time nudging Tilghman to take seriously the matter of his own salvation.

A copy of James's eloquent letter was included in *The Fugitive Blacksmith*, and much of the letter is as follows:

> *Dear Sir:*
>
> *It is now, as you are aware, about seventeen years since I left your house and service, at the age of twenty. Up to that time, I was, according to your rule and claim, your slave. Till the age of seven years, I was, of course, of little or no service to you. At that age, however, you hired me out, and for three years I earned my support; at the age of ten years, you took me to your place again, and in a short time after you*

put me to work at the blacksmith's trade, at which, together with the carpentering trade, etc., I served you peaceably until the day I left you, with exception of the short time you had sold me. . .for $700.

It is important for me to say to you that I have no consciousness of having done you any wrong. I called you master when I was with you from the mere force of circumstances; but I never regarded you as my master. The nature which God gave me did not allow me to believe that you had any more right to me than I had to you, and that was just none at all. And from an early age, I had intentions to free myself from your claim. I never consulted anyone about it; I had not advisers or instigators; I kept my own counsel entirely concealed in my own bosom. I never meditated any evil to your person or property, but I regarded you as my oppressor, and I deemed it my duty to get out of your hands by peaceable means.

I was always obedient to your commands. I labored for you diligently at all times. I acted with fidelity in any matter which you entrusted me. As you sometimes saw fit to entrust me with considerable money, to buy tools or materials, not a cent was ever coveted or kept.

During the time I served you in the capacity of blacksmith, your materials were used economically, your work was done expeditiously, and in the very best style, a style second to no [blacksmith] in your neighborhood. In short, sir, you well know that my habits from early life were advantageous to you. Drinking, gambling, fighting, etc., were not my habits. . . .

But what treatment did you see fit to return me for all this? You, in the most unfeeling manner, abused my father for no cause but speaking a word to you, as a man would speak to his fellowman, for the sake simply of a better understanding.

You vexed my mother, and because she, as a tender mother would do, showed solicitude for the virtue of her daughters, you threatened her in an insulting, brutal manner.

You abused my brother and sister without cause, and in like manner you did to myself; you surmised evil against me. You struck me with your walking-cane, called me insulting names, threatened me, swore at me, and became more and more wrathy in your conduct, and the time I quitted your place, I had good reason to believe that you were meditating serious evil against me.

Since I have been out of your hands, I have been signally favored of God, whence I infer that in leaving you, I acted strictly in accordance with His holy will. I have a conscience void of offence towards God and towards all men, yourself not excepted. And I verily believe that I have performed a sacred duty to God and myself, and a kindness to you, in taking the blood of my soul peaceably off your soul.

And now, dear sir, having spoken somewhat pointedly, I would, to convince you of my perfect good will towards you, in the most kind and respectful terms, remind you of your coming destiny. You are now over seventy years of age, pressing on to eternity with the weight of these seventy years upon you. Is not this enough without the blood of some half-score of souls?

You are aware that your right to property in man is now disputed by the civilized world. You are fully aware, also, that the question, whether the

Bible sanctions slavery has distinctly divided this nation in sentiment. On the side of biblical anti-slavery, we have many of the most learned, wise, and holy men in the land. If the Bible affords no sanction to slavery, (and I claim that it cannot), then it must be a sin of the deepest dye; and can you, sir, think to go to God in hope with a sin of such magnitude upon your soul?

. . .What, my dear sir, is a reputation among posterity, who are but worms, compared with a destiny in the world of spirits? And it is in light of that destiny that I would now have you look at this subject. . . . You will pardon me then for pressing this point in earnest good faith. You should, at this stage, review your life. . . and remember that you are soon to meet those whom you have held, and do hold in slavery, at the awful bar of the impartial Judge of all who doeth right. Then what will become of your own doubtful claims? What will be done with those doubts that agitated your mind years ago; will you answer for threatening, swearing, and using the cowhide among your slaves?

What will become of those long groans and unsatisfied complaints of your slaves, for vexing them with insulting words, placing them in the power of dogish and abusive overseers, or under your stripling, misguided, hotheaded son, to drive and whip at pleasure, and for selling parts or whole families to Georgia? They will all meet you at that bar. . . . Sir, I shall meet you there. The account between us for the first twenty years of my life will have definite character upon which one or the other will be able to make out a case.

Upon such a review as this, sir, you will, I am quite sure, see the need of seriousness. I assure you that the thought of meeting you in eternity, and before the dread tribunal of God, with a complaint in my mouth against you, is to me of the most weighty and solemn character. . . . What excuse could you offer at the bar of God?

. . .I can only say then, dear sir, farewell, till I meet you at the bar of God, where Jesus, who died for us, will judge between us. Now His blood can wash out our stain, break down the middle wall of partition, and reconcile us not only to God but to each other, then the word of His mouth, the sentence will set us as one. As for myself, I am quite ready to meet you face-to-face at the bar of God. I have done you no wrong; I have nothing to fear when we both fall into the hands of the just God.

I beseech you, dear sir, to look well and consider this matter soundly. In yonder world you can have no slaves—you can be no man's master—you can neither sell, buy, or whip, or drive. Are you then, by sustaining the relation of a slaveholder, forming a character to dwell with God in peace?

With kind regards, I am, sir, yours respectfully. . . .
                                        J. W. C. Pennington

There is no record of Frisby Tilghman's response.

NINE

Throughout the adult years of his life, James W. C. Pennington gained recognition on both sides of the Atlantic as a leading abolitionist, a powerful speaker, and an effective fund-raiser for the cause of freeing slaves. He was a prolific writer, contributing numerous essays to newspapers, and he was active on behalf of slaves in both the Underground Railroad and the New York Committee of Vigilance.

Ever a passionate advocate for education, he continued to teach school to African-Americans. He also continued to feel keenly the spiritual darkness that was too often part of the life of slave and former slave, and on that subject, he spoke and wrote often. He was also a strong proponent for evangelism.

He was remarried in 1848 to a woman named Elmira Way, though not much else is known about that marriage. It is documented that James moved around geographically, something that was an oddity in the nineteenth century with its slow transportation and limited lines of communication. It was as if the sensitive ex-fugitive never felt completely at home anywhere. He lived in New York, in the New England states, and even overseas in England before finally moving to the Deep South to perform missions work.

Though he pastored churches for the rest of his life, James's denominational associations became erratic as the years went by. He jumped from church to church—even from denomination to denomination—until 1864 when he joined the African Methodist Episcopal (A.M.E.) Church. Under its jurisdiction, he performed missions work in Natchez, Mississippi, for a short time and eventually was given a mission assignment in Jacksonville, Florida.

Though James's personal life in his later years was not well documented, what information does exist indicates that he fell into misfortune toward the end of his life. Perhaps it was loneliness. Perhaps he was ill, or maybe aging was not kind to him. Perhaps, like many Old Testament heroes, James Pennington was simply a flawed human being. Whatever the reasons, toward the end of his life, he struggled with alcoholism and antisocial behavior. One of his congregations even asked him to resign.

He lived long enough to celebrate the end of the bloody Civil War and the emancipation of slaves in the United States. Then in October 1870, James W. C. Pennington, former slave, brilliant essayist and autobiographer, leading abolitionist, and minister of God died in Florida in poverty and neglect. None of his relatives were present when he died. In spite of his stature as a leader of his people, none of the African-American press noted his passing. He left no children that we know of to carry on his name. In fact, his name has been almost forgotten by history.

Almost forgotten, but not quite—because James W. C.

Pennington wrote his remarkable book which can still be read today, over 150 years after its initial publication. *The Fugitive Blacksmith* showed the world then and now the courage of one young man who had to be free from bondage—physically, emotionally, and spiritually—or he would surely perish. Through the help of his beloved Creator, James W. C. Pennington did become a free man—in every way—and an inspiration to the people of his time and ours.

Harriet
TUBMAN

ONE

It was Christmas afternoon in Maryland, 1854. Inside the rough log cabin, a fire crackled in the fireplace. An old slave woman sat next to it, gazing into the flames. Every now and then she heaved a sigh.

Earlier in the day, the fire had roared as the old woman cooked a huge and tasty Christmas dinner in its flames for her grown children. She had assumed they would come home from the other plantations where they lived to spend the holiday with her husband and her, the same as they had every year on one of the few days slaves did not have to work. She'd killed and roasted a pig and cooked up her children's favorite foods. Then she waited all day for them. Even her husband had taken to looking out the door from time to time.

But not one of her children or grandchildren had come. Dusk was falling, and it was clear they weren't coming at all. It was almost more than the old woman could bear. She rocked back and forth and wept quietly. What she could not know was that some of those children were no more than a few yards away, hiding in a shed filled with fodder for livestock, waiting for darkness to fall. On this night, they planned to escape their lives of slavery.

One daughter, Harriet, the youngest of ten children born to the aging Ben and Harriet Ross, secretly watched her mother through the open cabin door. Firelight made the old woman's face bright, and Harriet could see she was crying. Harriet was heartbroken that she could not speak to her mother directly.

For five years now, Harriet had secretly spirited slaves north to freedom, and tomorrow she would be taking more, her own kin, out of Maryland. They had decided to all come say good-bye, but once they had gotten closer to their mother, Harriet realized that the emotional good-byes would be noticed. And that would jeopardize all their lives, including the lives of their parents. So the escaping slaves hid nearby instead.

Harriet wished they could have celebrated Christmas all together with the old folks. But Christmas on the plantation also meant a few rare days of no work, and if she could get her runaways on their way soon, they could be long gone by the time they were missed and well on the road to freedom. For now, they hid in the shed, resting up for a long, dangerous journey, which would be made mostly on foot through parts of Maryland, Delaware, New Jersey, and into Pennsylvania.

Two of the men, John and Peter, were not related to Harriet, and once darkness fell, they knocked at the cabin door of the old folks to ask for food. Old Poppa Ross came to the door and stepped outside to talk to the men.

Outside, the men spoke softly. "We're friends of Harriet's and your boys," they told Poppa Ross. "They didn't come to you 'cause we're heading north. We're in the shed over yonder right now, and your children want to say good-bye. And we need food real bad."

The old man understood immediately. Calmly, he slipped back into the cabin and spoke to his wife, not telling her that her children were nearby. Then he bundled up some food in a gunnysack and followed the other men away from the cabin.

When they got close to the shed, Poppa Ross said, "Blindfold me."

The younger men looked at each other. Was this old man crazy?

"I say blindfold me, and make it tight, young fellas."

One man pulled out his bandanna, rolled it into a long strip, and tied it over the old man's eyes. Then they led him into the shed where his children were hiding.

Harriet and her brothers spent time with their father that Christmas Day. They ate and talked together, but the old man never took off his blindfold. That night, rested and carrying food for the journey, Harriet and her fugitives headed north.

Old Poppa Ross knew that when his children were dis-covered missing, he would be questioned, and Poppa was a devout Christian who would not lie. And sure enough, once the family members were discovered missing, he and his wife were called to the master's house, which everyone called the Big House, for questioning. Slaves were missing in the area, so the authorities had come to question the Rosses about their children.

Of course, Momma Ross knew nothing. "I looked for them all day," she said sadly. "They never did come."

"Did you see your children before they left, old man?" the law asked Poppa.

"No," he said. "I ain't seen my children in months."

And it was true. He had talked to his children; he had eaten with them. But he did not "see" them before they escaped to freedom. And he knew he might never see any of them again.

But meanwhile he had the great satisfaction of knowing that his baby daughter, now all grown up into the courageous Harriet Tubman, slowly and with the assurance of one watched over by the Lord Himself escorted three more of Poppa Ross's own blood into the land of Canada. There they would be slaves no more.

And one day Harriet was coming back.

TWO

A layer of fog settled over the saltwater marshes of eastern Maryland. Moving slowly through the silver haze was a wagon drawn by one beaten-down old horse. A young white woman held the reins, and tucked in the back sat a small slave girl, little Minty Ross, age six. She shivered in her sack dress in the damp fog. Her soft brown eyes blinked in terror, for Minty had just been sold.

Not an hour ago she'd been dragged crying from the arms of her momma and poppa back at the only home she'd ever known on the land of Edward Brodas in Dorchester County. Now she was on her way to this stranger's house. The white woman needed some kind of help in the house, but she was not well off enough to afford an adult slave. The only slave she and her husband could afford to buy was a child—Minty.

Where on earth was she being taken? The child's mind conjured up horrible scenes, some possible, some not, things she'd heard about back in the slave quarters when people whispered at night. Were white people really ghosts? Would they beat her? Kill her? Her heart pounded in dread.

In these years, the entire Southern way of life in the United States was dependent upon the institution of slavery. The huge plantations of the wealthier Southerners grew acres and acres of cotton and tobacco, and these plantations needed hundreds of people to work the land, raise the live-stock, and run the kitchen and the rest of the master's house. Those hundreds—thousands—of people were black slaves.

A slave owned nothing, not even himself. Slaves were bought and sold as if they were animals. They were depen-dent upon the generosity of the master to feed, clothe, and house them in one-room shacks with dirt floors and no windows. Most slaves had one outfit to wear—one dress or one pair of pants and one shirt.

Slaves could not simply come and go as they pleased. They needed permission to travel from place to place, and even congregating in the slave quarters was frowned upon. Every now and then slaves would run away, and then they were tracked down with dogs. If they successfully escaped, they were never seen again. If they were found, they were whipped severely to punish them and to make an example of them so that others would be too frightened to try the same thing. The life of a slave was full of uncertainty, because if the fields did not produce and the master of the plantation did not prosper, he might sell some slaves for extra cash. Black families were torn apart this way on a regular basis.

This is the life that little Minty—one day to be known as Harriet Tubman—was born into, and now she was the one being ripped from her family.

She was born around 1820, though no record was made of the actual date of her birth. She was named Araminta Ross—it would be years before she was called Harriet—and her birth was most welcome. Her mother had already lost two small daughters who were sold to a chain gang, and she fiercely wished to have and protect this baby daughter.

No doubt there would be a grim future ahead for baby Minty since slave life was so hard. But the slaves themselves found ways to live their hard existence with a certain amount of joy. One way was their love and concern for one another, and another way was their love for God. Their sorrows, their hopes, and their aspirations were expressed in worship to Him and in song.

On some plantations, slaves were allowed to gather for church. Other plantations found any gathering at all too threatening—the slaves, they feared, would be planning escape or, even worse, the murder of their masters. On those plantations, slaves would worship in secret in what they called brush arbors—areas of dense pine boughs that would absorb sound. Even fear of the whip did not keep them from praising Jesus out loud.

Today Minty looked up at the pearl-gray sky. She took comfort in the knowledge that her mother was praying for her at this very minute. She'd heard her mother pray fervently in the privacy of their cabin every time a slave disappeared. Then she would rock and moan. It was kind of like singing, but it was softer, and it seemed full of all the hurt in the world.

Today, at age six, Minty suddenly understood her mother's prayers and moans in a way she did not even the day before. She thought of the songs she'd heard sung in the slave quarters, songs the masters had decided were dangerous and might cause a slave to think evil thoughts about his master. At first Minty had not been able to figure that out. How could it be evil to sing about wanting to go to Glory and be with Jesus?

And what was wrong with singing about the stories in the Bible? Since slaves rarely could read, Bible stories were told aloud and sung about. Minty loved the songs about Moses leading the Israelites out of Egypt through all kinds of dangers to get to the Promised Land, especially her favorite song, which went:

> Go down, Moses,
> Way down in Egypt land.
> Tell ole Pharaoh
> Let my people go!

Sometimes the songs were sung softly in the cabin, and sometimes the field hands sang them loud and strong and in unison. She knew what they were about—a day would come when Jesus would come again to take them away and make everything right. When the lion would lie down with the lamb. When there would no longer be such a thing as slavery.

Because even as a little slip of a girl, Minty understood that slavery was evil. Some Christian masters read their Bibles differently on that topic, and white folks all over the world discussed to no end whether or not slavery should continue to exist. But slaves knew God had never intended them to be enslaved in the first place.

Minty had been a little too young to understand that the songs she loved had a second meaning to many slaves. These songs often told of being freed from slavery by dying and going on to heaven, but sometimes they told about taking the actual journey north to liberty. Minty would hear someone sing, "Oh Canaan, sweet Canaan, I am bound for the land of Canaan," and the sweet sounds seemed full of mystery to her. She had only recently been able to tell apart the words Canaan and Canada, they felt so alike rolled on her Southern tongue. She learned that Canaan was the Promised Land in the Bible, whereas Canada was a snowy land way up north where there was no slavery whatsoever. Were they really the same place, she wondered?

As the wagon pulled onto another dirt road, Minty grew numb with cold and fear. A small log house appeared in a clearing in the woods, and she could smell a river nearby. Otherwise, Minty had no idea where she was. She'd never left the Brodas Plantation in her whole young life.

THREE

At her new home, Minty was expected to help the young mistress, Mrs. Cook, with her work. Mrs. Cook was a weaver who worked on a loom and a spinning wheel inside the house, and Mr. Cook trapped fish and hunted animals for a living. The Cooks owned very little land and were not at all wealthy, but their log house was the biggest one Minty had ever been in, since she'd never set foot in the Big House back home.

The Cooks' cabin had more than one room, but Minty was expected to sleep on the floor next to the kitchen fireplace as if she were a dog. The Cooks fed her about as much as they'd feed a dog, too—not much at all. They intended to spend as little money as possible on this extra mouth in the house.

Minty's job was to wind yarn while Mrs. Cook worked the loom and wheel. Minty wasn't very good at the task, and she sneezed all the time from getting the yarn fuzz in her nose and mouth. It didn't help that she was frightened and homesick and usually hungry.

Mrs. Cook scolded Minty constantly, but it didn't seem to improve Minty's work. Finally she handed the child over to Mr. Cook. "See if she's any help to you outside. She's no use to me."

Mr. Cook taught Minty to watch his trap lines in the river while he hunted elsewhere. Minty watched for muskrats which would be sold for their fur, and she hauled them out of the river in trap cages. Although it was cold in and around the river, she was relieved to be out of the house and off by herself. She'd learned to appreciate God's natural world from her father, who was by far the smartest man Minty knew.

Poppa Ross could predict weather for the next day or the next season simply by watching the sky or observing animals in the woods. He knew which herbs and plants were poisonous and which were for healing. He understood the phases of the moon and how they impacted farming and fishing. He knew the constellations, and he taught them all to his daughter. In particular, he pointed out the North Star. He taught her that it held a special meaning: The North Star led to freedom.

Now early in the dark morning, Minty could still see that North Star. She knew her parents were watching that same star, and she took comfort in that thought. She took to looking up at the sky a lot because, like those river muskrats she hauled in, Minty felt trapped.

One day she came down with the measles. These were days when such illnesses could kill a child, but the Cooks made her continue to work in spite of her fever, wading barefoot in the cold river, hauling in the heavy baskets of trapped animals. The fever increased, and Minty developed bronchitis on top of her measles. Eventually she simply collapsed.

The Cooks wrapped her in a blanket and left her alone.

Slaves had an amazing network of communication. It was long known and accepted that the slave quarters knew the happenings in the Big House before the inhabitants of the Big House did. And news about slaves themselves traveled rapidly from plantation to plantation. Consequently, word about how sick Minty was traveled to the Brodas Plantation. Momma Ross went to Mr. Brodas and begged to have her child back so she could nurse her back to health herself.

Brodas relented and sent for Mr. Cook and Minty. "Let her people make her well," he told Mr. Cook. "I don't know how they do it, but they do. Then I'll send her back to you."

Cook was relieved. If Minty died, he would lose his investment, so he agreed wholeheartedly to the plan. He left Minty with Brodas.

Minty was carried back to her parents' cabin where she was slowly nursed back to health by her parent with herbs and food. Eventually she recovered enough to go back to the Cook house.

Bronchitis at such a young age forever affected her voice. It became deep and husky, unusual for a child. She retained that distinct voice into adulthood, and it was to come in very handy when she would visit slave quarters in the night. Then she would be recognized in the dark by the sound of it in song. She wouldn't have to identify herself any other way.

But for now, back at the Cooks', things were even worse than before since it was decided Minty should stay indoors. But she was just as clumsy at weaving work as she had been before. It wasn't long before the Cooks gave up on her and took her back to Brodas, telling him she was stupid. They certainly were not going to keep feeding someone who wouldn't work.

Minty was grateful to be back playing in the slave

quarters. But even at the age of seven, she would be expected to work. All slaves worked from the time they were old enough to leave their mothers, the littlest ones carrying water to the field hands. Earning their keep was their only survival.

Momma and Poppa Ross were worried that Minty had become too much of a problem for the master and that he might sell her off. He'd done it before, and they didn't think they could bear that again, especially with their youngest and smartest child, Minty.

Word was out in the slave communication network that the time was ripe for another big slave sale on the plantation. To keep up his standard of living, Brodas needed money. When the crops weren't good—and they weren't lately—he sold timber from his forest. And slaves. More and more plantations were supporting themselves from raising and selling slaves instead of crops. And the chain gang kept coming around, threatening to take more people out of the quarters.

But little Minty didn't go with the chain gang. The master sold her once more, this time to a Miss Susan. Minty moved to the woman's house to work as a babysitter and housekeeper. Still a child herself, she was expected to take care of Miss Susan's only child—a baby. Minty was too small to hold the baby, so she would sit on the floor cross-legged and place the baby in her lap. This way, she became a living cradle for the baby, holding it in her lap all day unless Miss Susan was feeding it.

At night the baby went into an actual cradle, and Minty slept on the floor next to it. Or, rather, didn't sleep. She was expected to rock the cradle any time this especially fussy baby cried so it would go back to sleep. She learned how to rock the cradle constantly and at the same time doze.

Keeping house for Miss Susan was a nightmare. Minty

had only lived in log cabins all her young years, and she had never even seen polished furniture and carved wood and carpets such as this house had. Minty had grown up with a dirt floor, and even at the Cooks', she had slept next to ashes in the fireplace. So when Miss Susan told her to dust, Minty had no clue as to what that meant. She didn't even know what questions to ask.

Miss Susan was not a patient or kind woman, and one day she brought out a whip. She whacked Minty with it, calling her "stupid." Fortunately, Miss Susan's sister intervened and scolded her sister for using the whip on a child. Then the sister herself taught Minty how to clean a house.

But Miss Susan was still quick to use that whip. If the baby cried, she whipped Minty. If anything went wrong in the house, she whipped Minty. If Miss Susan was simply in a bad mood, she whipped Minty. When one day Miss Susan caught Minty sneaking a lump of sugar from the sugar bowl, out came the whip. This time, Minty couldn't take it anymore, and she ran. Miss Susan and her husband chased her, but they eventually gave up.

Minty stayed away as long as she could stand it, hiding for several days in a pigpen and fighting the pigs for their food. She had no idea how to get back to her parents; she didn't know any more about where she was geographically than she'd known back at the Cooks'. There wasn't even a river nearby here.

Eventually, hungry and filthy, she dragged herself back to the house. As she feared would happen, she was whipped, more severely this time, after which the couple took her back to Brodas. They gave him the same complaint the Cooks had given—that Minty was stupid.

Brodas once again turned Minty over to her mother, this time to heal up the bleeding whip marks that lay on top of older whipping scars.

Momma Ross was angry, but she only expressed it in the cabin, sometimes to Poppa, sometimes to the Lord. She sponged cool, herbal teas onto Minty's back and neck while Minty slept on her stomach. For days she slept, letting her wounds heal and making up for all that sleep she'd lost rocking the white baby's cradle and fighting with hungry pigs. Her mother's comforting voice moved into Minty's dreams, and she knew, even asleep, that she was safe.

While Minty was getting her strength back, Brodas let Momma Ross know that he was going to "hire out" Minty. Sometimes rather than sell a slave, a slaveholder might hire out the slave's work to someone else for cash. Momma Ross was certainly pleased that Minty could continue living at home, but she was concerned about the hiring out. She had hoped Minty could learn a useful indoor trade so that she could become a house slave and live a marginally easier life than a field slave. But Brodas had decided to make Minty, a child not yet ten years of age, a field hand.

It was going to make all the difference in the world.

FOUR

Minty became a field hand, hired out to other farmers for cash for Brodas. Though she never grew over five feet tall, she was amazingly strong. Her skinny frame filled out so that now she had not only the slight curves of a young woman, but she also had visible muscles in her arms, legs, and shoulders—muscles which hardened like a man's. Her back grew straight and strong. Her bare feet and her hard-working hands toughened with calluses. Besides her physical strength, her knowledge of animals and all things outdoors helped her in her new work.

At the age of eleven, Minty decided she was no longer a child. She stopped wearing the sack garment children wore and began wearing a woman's dress. She managed to twist the skirt of it into something like trousers when necessary in the field. She also wore a colorful bandanna tied around her head like the other grown women.

Minty was expected to lift, pick, push, and plow like a man. And she rose to the occasion, because she loved to be outdoors. She could breathe in fresh air instead of wool lint or soiled diapers. She could study the landscape, the birds, the river. She could join her fellow workers in song that would rise over the fields and the trees and go straight on up to Jesus. Every day of being outdoors made Minty pray with gratitude. What Momma had thought was all wrong on the master's part had actually been right for Minty. The Lord's hand was in that, she knew.

Slaves were not allowed to have conversations while working, and overseers on horseback carried whips to enforce that rule. But slaves were adept at keeping track of the overseers' whereabouts and communicating with each other quietly. On one such occasion, Minty first heard reference to the Underground Railroad.

She was puzzled as she listened to someone tell of a slave who was no longer around. "He's on that underground railroad and never coming back," the field hand said with a quiet satisfaction.

Minty kept her hands moving, but her mind moved even faster. What was the field hand talking about? She'd seen trains. At night she could hear their sad, faraway whistles from miles away.

But a train under the ground?

It took some time and a lot of whispering, but eventually Minty sorted out what the Underground Railroad was. It was, first of all, not a railroad, nor was it under the ground. It seemed there were white people, mostly up North but some down South, who did not believe in slavery. These people were Quakers who talked with "thee" and "thou" in their speech, and Methodists, and Europeans now living in America, the land of the free. These people of faith knew without a doubt that God had made all humans equal. They also knew that the Constitution of the United States confirmed it. And they were willing to risk their lives for what was moral and right. They actively fought the evil of slavery by helping slaves escape to the North.

Minty had never heard of such white people. She certainly had never known any like that herself. Miss Susan's sister had shown her a little compassion, but that was unusual. Could it be true that such white folks existed?

Yes, she was told by the others in the fields. Lots of them. And freed blacks were involved, too. She learned that there were routes all over the nation that slaves could travel to get to free soil. Most of the travel was on foot, she learned, and there were code words all along the way. A "station" was a house that would provide shelter, food, and money. Runaway slaves were called "passengers," and there were "conductors" along the way, citizens to guide them. Once the runaways got to freedom in the Northern states, there were plenty of freed blacks and concerned whites committed to freedom to help them start life over in a strange land.

This sounded more like a railroad in heaven to Minty than a railroad here on earth. But her people assured her this Underground Railroad truly existed, even in the very state of Maryland. You simply had to know the right white person to get started and have the nerve to take off.

Know white people? Minty thought when she heard this. And trust white people? She shook her head. How could she trust a race of people who beat her and sold her? That would be plain foolish. She was sure of it.

By her thirteenth year, Minty was as strong as or stronger than any man on the plantation. She was also short and slim and female, which led Master Brodas and his overseers to feel not the least bit threatened by her. Judging by her hard work, lack of chatter, and full-voiced singing in the fields, Brodas called Minty "a good slave." But he could not know what was going on inside her mind. Minty knew what was right and what was wrong. And she knew it was wrong for her—and all of her people—not to be free. The pressure of bondage was swelling up inside her.

One harvest during a corn shucking, Minty noticed a slave acting oddly. She glanced around, still shucking corn, to see if anyone else noticed. The slave was shucking too slowly and seemed nervous and jumpy. That was never a way to act around an overseer. Fortunately, the overseer had his back to the slave.

Suddenly Minty saw the slave blast out of the crowd and run. He was halfway across a field before the overseer noticed and took off after him, whip in hand. Usually overseers sat on a horse to intimidate the workers and to move quickly. But this overseer was on foot and hadn't stopped to mount his horse. Without thinking, Minty took off after the overseer and the slave.

She found both men in a building. The overseer threatened to whip the slave immediately, and when he saw Minty, he ordered her to tie up the man so the whipping could commence. Minty did nothing, simply stood and watched, until the slave darted past her, back out the door. The overseer headed for the doorway after him, but Minty stood solidly blocking his way.

The overseer grabbed a two-pound brick and threw it after the escaping slave, but the throw was too short to hit the slave. He got away, but the brick hit Minty square in the forehead, knocking her clean out. She collapsed in a pool of her own blood.

Once again, Minty was taken to her parents' cabin, where she was stretched out on a pallet on the floor, this time lapsing in and out of consciousness, near death. The brick had cracked her skull, and there was an ugly, frightening hole in her forehead. She slept and slept. Even when she was sort of awake, she dozed off and on. For months Momma Ross worked on her daughter's wound, dressing it with herbs, while she worried and prayed over her semi-conscious child.

Word of Minty's brave and selfless act helping the slave get away spread quickly, and out of admiration for her, the slave community changed her name. They would no longer call her by her baby name; from now on, she would be called by her mother's name, Harriet. It was a way people in the quarters could show their respect for one of their own without actually speaking about her act of outright rebellion. It was a tremendous honor.

Now there were two questions on everyone's lips. Would young Harriet survive, and, if she did, what would the master do with her? It didn't look like she was going to live, much less return to being the strong young woman she was before the injury. Certainly nobody would buy her if she wasn't whole and able to work. And if a slave couldn't work, well, that was a real problem for that slave.

Young Harriet's mother prayed hard. November passed, then Christmas. Harriet was unable to speak or walk. Winter came and went.

Finally as spring approached and the rest of the world woke up from its dormant state, so did Harriet. She stayed quiet for many more weeks, but she was conscious. The wound was now a nasty scar.

Miraculously, Harriet would live.

FIVE

The master heard Harriet was recovering, and he tried to sell her again, but prospective buyers only laughed at him. All they could see was a physically weak woman, obviously rebellious, and frightening to look at with that scar on her forehead. No one was going to pay money for a slave with problems.

Though Harriet was on the mend, she now had horrible headaches. Even the scar itself was painful. She was prone to passing out, and she never knew when she would fall into a deep sleep. She had no control over it at all. She could be in the middle of a sentence or standing by the door, and she would simply collapse on the ground, sound asleep. She could not be awakened when it happened; it was very much like being in a coma.

During the deep sleep, she would sometimes have visions so vivid and detailed that often her visions seemed more real than her actual surroundings. She floated in and out of the real world and the world inside her mind.

As Harriet's body repaired, she came to believe that she had been spared—and even changed—for a reason. At first she thought the reason was to pray for Master Brodas, and she spent days in prayer, asking God to work on Brodas and convert him. For weeks Harriet lay quietly on her pallet, often deep in prayer for the white master.

She never would know if Brodas became converted, since that was between him and God. But she did learn that he was arranging the sale of two of Harriet's brothers and Harriet herself. They would leave with the next chain gang and head farther south. Harriet was truly frightened. She would never survive the trip, that she knew. And she was too sick to run away.

A dark anger moved into Harriet's heart. She began praying that God would kill Brodas. It became like a steady beat inside her throbbing head: Kill him, Lord. Kill him. She became obsessed with hatred for the man. A few days later, Brodas became suddenly ill, and a few days after that, he died.

When Harriet learned of the master's death, she curled into a ball on her pallet in the cabin, her head pounding. She was horrified and guilt-stricken. Though she wanted to believe otherwise, she believed that her prayers had killed Edward Brodas, and she was filled with remorse. The day would come eventually when Harriet would realize that God did not strike Brodas dead based on her prayers, but she vowed never again to pray that evil befall another human being. Now she prayed for forgiveness for herself and for God to help her do good in this world.

After the master of any plantation died, there was concern among the slaves. What would the heirs do with them? It wasn't unusual for an heir to sell slaves off. But fortunately, in this case, the heir, a doctor and minister, decided not to sell any slaves outside the state of Maryland. For a while everyone breathed a little easier.

Harriet recovered enough to perform housework tasks, and she was hired out to a man named Stewart. After a short while, she appealed to Stewart to let her work outside. She assured him she was strong and good with an ax, so Stewart agreed to let her be a field hand. Just as she had in the past, Harriet produced as much work as a man, and because she was a woman, Stewart didn't have to pay as much for her labor.

Harriet was so unnaturally strong that Stewart would sometimes invite his friends over to watch her lift and throw heavy items. For his friends' entertainment, Stewart even had Harriet haul a barge down the river all by herself wearing a harness connected to the barge as she walked along the shore. His friends loved the show, but Harriet felt like an animal doing tricks.

The good news, however, was that Stewart allowed Harriet to hire herself out in her free time and make a little money for herself. Now Harriet was often allowed to work with her Poppa Ross cutting down timber. The beauty of this was that she could spend time with her wise father, who picked right up where he left off years ago teaching his daughter everything he knew about nature.

These lessons had an undercurrent of importance about them. They were not simply for fun and curiosity. Poppa Ross knew his daughter was too special not to be free. He knew someday, somehow, she would hit the road, and he might never see her again. But he wanted her to be free as much as she wanted to be. He hoped he could impart enough knowledge to her to allow her to escape successfully. Harriet sensed her father's unspoken motives. Poppa taught Harriet which herbs were medicinal and how to use them for healing purposes. He taught her which roots and berries were edible. He taught her about the river and the marshes and all the geography of Maryland he knew, information he had picked up over the years when he had accompanied Brodas on trips.

Most important, without talking about it at all, Poppa Ross taught Harriet how to move quietly in the woods without making a sound. He once told her that a forest is a noisy thing when you listen to it. Ever since the Fall in the Garden of Eden, the perfect beauty in God's world was still amazing but also stained. This stain disturbed the peace and made noise. Harriet listened to twigs break, birds call, owls hoot, deer scamper, rabbits scurry, and branches crash to the forest floor.

As Poppa Ross taught Harriet how to listen to sounds and interpret them, he also showed her how to mimic hoot owls and birds. He taught her to listen to her own forest noises. Then he showed her how to eliminate them. She became so good at moving through the forest silently that she could even sneak up and startle her old father. He was pleased. Hopeful and pleased.

For several years life went on without any serious problems in the Ross family. Harriet continued to work hard and hire herself out for some money of her own. But as she moved into her twenties, Harriet found that something in her life was missing. She found herself listening to the mourning doves and their plaintive songs. "Mourning dove crying for rain," Momma Ross had always told her. But the field hands said, "Mourning dove crying for its mate."

A mate. A husband. That's what was missing. Harriet was aware of soft new feelings—a desire to marry a good man, maybe have children. For the first time, she shyly observed the men around her in a different light. She wondered who might make a suitable husband.

When a man called John Tubman noticed Harriet, she knew her quest for love was finished. Serious young Harriet found a balance to her somber personality in this handsome, laughing man. Maybe the fact that John was a free man made him that much more appealing. At any rate, Harriet fell in love.

Slaves didn't have actual weddings or even legal marriages in the manner of whites. But slaves did have a marriage ceremony called "jumping the broom." Slaves who wished to marry asked permission of the master, and if he agreed to the union, the betrothed and their families would gather around a broom lying on the floor. Then the couple would jump together over the broom, symbolizing their commitment to a future together. Sometimes if the master was a more devout Christian man, he would make certain there was a religious ceremony for the new couple.

In 1844, whether it was by a religious ceremony or jumping the broom, Harriet Ross became John Tubman's wife. She left her parents' cabin and moved in with her new husband.

SIX

There was one thing that troubled Harriet Tubman about her new marriage. She was still a slave. John Tubman's slave parents had been freed after the death of their master, which sometimes happened, and that event had made John a free man. But even though Harriet was now the wife of a free man, she was still a slave.

There was no security in this state of existence. Harriet's entire family were slaves. Any one of them—including Harriet—could be sold at the whim of their owners, and if that happened, those separations could very well be forever. Harriet loved John, and it was particularly painful for her to realize that if one day she were sold, she might never see her husband or any of her family members again.

The Underground Railroad continued to flourish, and Harriet continued to hear amazing stories about runaways. She yearned for freedom more than anything, and she was realizing more and more that her only hope of having freedom was to flee north. She shared her hopes with her husband, suggesting they run away together and start over in the North.

John Tubman, usually good-natured, became very agitated. Why did Harriet find it so necessary to be free? Why would she jeopardize everything they'd worked for? Why would she risk their very lives?

This kind of thinking shocked Harriet. "You're free, John," she said. "Don't you want that for me? Don't you want children someday and have them be free?"

"We're all right just the way we are," John responded. "I make my own money, and you're able to hire out for money, too. We got our own place. We aren't so bad off."

But things weren't all that good, either. Times were hard on the plantation. Cotton prices were going down, and everyone knew what that meant—more slaves would be sold to the chain gangs. Harriet had come close to being sold to a chain gang before, and if that came to be, there would be nothing John could do about it. She appealed to him again. "Please, John, I know there's a way out. Slaves run north all the time and make it. We could, too. Then nobody would ever be able to separate us."

But John Tubman simply shook his head.

Harriet started having a series of dreams at night. In them, she could see and hear the terrors of slaves being rousted out of their cabins at night and sold. She could see and hear the chain gang trudging, their irons clanking, the slaves weeping.

Then she dreamed she was swimming across a river. Just as she was about to go down in the deep water and drown, women dressed in white reached out, grabbed her flailing arms, and pulled her across.

She decided the first dream was a warning from God that she was going to be sold, and the second dream was a comfort from God, that should she head north; His angels would watch over her. She approached John Tubman again about running away by telling him about the dreams.

First he laughed at her. Then he became angry. He bent down and put his face close to hers and said, "If you run, I'll tell the master."

Harriet was stunned. "You know what they do to runaways," she said. "You would let them do that to me?"

"Try running and see," he said. She looked deep into his eyes and saw no love there. For the first time, Harriet was afraid of John.

This was a terrible hurt that her own husband would threaten to betray her to the master—a betrayal that could cost her her very life.

But Harriet needed to be free. And she believed the Lord wanted to help her be free, always had known it, and she believed that if John could see clearly, he'd want the same. She was certain that the time would come when he would see freedom as something his wife must have. But that time was not now.

Harriet became more determined to leave as soon as possible. Now she needed not only to watch for the right time to escape, she also had to observe John closely so that he would not know. She did not doubt for a minute that he would turn on her.

By 1849 enough time had elapsed without Harriet leaving that John no longer seemed suspicious. Harriet noted it and was relieved. But it wasn't yet time to leave.

One day a white woman approached Harriet while she was working in the fields near the road. Harriet had never looked at white people's faces much. In the South, blacks did not look whites in the eyes, and Harriet found their faces frightening anyway. They seemed to have no insides, no warmth.

But she found herself looking directly at the white woman. She was old and had the kindest face Harriet had ever seen, except for her own mother's. This old woman had straight, thin white hair parted neatly in the center, eyes as gray as a spring rain cloud, and soft-looking skin with blue veins showing at her temples. She wore a simple dress and bonnet, the clean and crisp attire of a farmer's wife.

The old woman reined in her horse and turned in her wagon to face Harriet. She smiled, looking right into Harriet's eyes, and began chatting about the day, the weather, the crops. The woman was so friendly and talkative that for the first time in Harriet's life, she found herself talking normally and naturally to someone who was not black. For several weeks, Harriet and the farmer's wife chatted a couple times per week there at the side of the road.

As feared, things started to change on the plantation. Slaves were being sold. Before anyone knew what was happening, two more of Harriet's own sisters were gone on the chain gang. Her parents were devastated. There was an air of panic all over the slave quarters.

Harriet found herself sharing the news with her new white friend. The woman quietly responded, "If you ever need anything, Harriet—anything at all—you know where I live."

Harriet nodded, and the old woman rode off on her wagon. Maybe, Harriet thought, just maybe the women dressed in white in the dreams represented white women instead of angels. One thing was certain: The time had come to leave.

Once Harriet decided to go north she found she was afraid to go alone. Though she obviously did not dare tell John, she did ask three of her brothers to go with her. They agreed to it.

On the night of their escape, Harriet waited until John was asleep; then she met her brothers near the fields. Off they went.

But after only a mile, her brothers' fears got the better of them. They insisted on going back. Furthermore, they forced their baby sister to return with them.

Harriet was angry with her brothers, and she realized that if she was going to escape, she'd have to do it alone. But it couldn't be tonight. She slipped back into her cabin, grateful that John was sound asleep and hadn't noticed she'd left.

Two days later a field hand told Harriet that he'd just learned the chain gang was taking her and her three brothers that very night. Now she knew she'd have to leave as soon as it was dark, and after her experience with her brothers earlier in the week, she knew she'd have to go alone.

There was plenty about the upcoming journey to frighten Harriet. The lack of food and shelter, the fact that she'd never traveled alone before, the need to travel only at night and stay hidden during the day, the threat of being hunted down by bloodhounds and returned to be whipped—all these were good reasons to be afraid.

But it was also her own body that Harriet had to consider. She was afraid it would betray her. Her prominent scar made her easily recognizable. She had an unusually lean yet muscular build for a woman, and nobody who ever heard her deep voice forgot it. Her headaches and blackouts could come at any time. She might be crossing a road, in full view, and have no control over falling into a deep sleep right there in the middle of the road. Or she could fall asleep while crossing a river and drown.

Nevertheless, Harriet felt God's assurance settle over her in the middle of her panic. She believed this journey was blessed.

That night Harriet rose in the dark and tied some food up in a kerchief. Then she left the cabin and John Tubman. It pained her deeply to leave her husband. But she felt she had no other choice; she simply could not be sold South, never to see any of her loved ones again.

She left the plantation by way of the back of the Big House where Harriet's sister was a cook. Because of the heat in the South and the heat of cooking, the kitchen on a plantation sat in a small, separate building a few steps from the Big House. Staying well outside the kitchen where her sister was working late, Harriet composed a song on the spot and sang it so the sister would know where she'd be:

> *Good-bye, I'm going to leave you,*
> *Good-bye, I'll meet you in the Kingdom. . . .*

And so Harriet set out for freedom.

SEVEN

At the time Harriet headed north, the states that were considered free territory for fugitive slaves were Connecticut, Illinois, Indiana, Maine, Massachusetts, Michigan, New Hampshire, New Jersey, New York, Ohio, Pennsylvania, Rhode Island, and Vermont. Eventually Minnesota and Iowa also became free states.

Harriet's destination was Philadelphia, Pennsylvania, where there was a network of freed slaves and other concerned people to help her start a new life. Fortunately, Maryland was fairly close to Pennsylvania, around ninety miles. But she would still have to travel many miles on foot.

Her first stop was the old white woman's house. She did not seem the least bit surprised to see Harriet. She sat Harriet down and explained the Underground Railroad more fully to her, then she wrote two names on a piece of paper.

"These are the next places for you to stop," she said. "You'll be safe there. I'll tell you how to get to the first one, and you show them this paper. They'll tell you how to get to the next stop."

Harriet said good-bye to the first white person she would call friend, and she headed for the woods in the dark of night, following the North Star.

That first frightening night, she used all the knowledge she had of the woods to get her through the dense trees and underbrush. She kept moving all night, quickly, quickly, knowing that every step was one more step away from bloodhounds and the whip. And somehow by the end of that first night, Harriet lost her fear. She had kept her wits about her, and her fear was gone, never to return in full measure. Years later, "fearless" was one of the words that everyone who knew Harriet would use to describe her.

The next morning she found the farmhouse the old woman had described. She handed her piece of paper to the woman who answered the kitchen door, and the woman smiled. "Come and eat," she said.

Harriet sat at the table and ate a country breakfast with fresh-baked biscuits. It was another new experience for Harriet, a slave all her life, to be fed by a white woman.

After breakfast, the woman handed her a broom and suggested she sweep the yard. Many people in the South had dirt yards that they would sweep into pretty patterns, and Harriet had swept yards before. At first it was hard for Harriet to relax out in the open, but she soon realized that the law would never suspect a black woman working right out in the open of being a runaway. She swept the yard happily.

Harriet left the farm that night on the floor of the farmer's produce wagon, covered with a blanket and a load of fresh vegetables. She thought wistfully about John and the rest of her family and what would be happening right now back home. She dozed and dreamed and marveled that the Lord had taken away her fear.

The wagon stopped at a river in the dark hours of early morning. The farmer gave Harriet her next instructions and some advice. "Travel only at night. And don't set foot on the road, ever." Then he wished her Godspeed. Harriet thanked him and proceeded to follow the river northward.

Harriet walked all night to the next designated stop, this time on the riverbank. Here another stranger greeted her calmly and kindly just like the first two white people had at their "stations," and he helped her climb into his boat. He rowed for several miles, miles that Harriet would have had to walk had this good man not been part of a network of kind Christians.

At the end of their journey, the man sent her on foot to another farm, where she was given a meal and a clever hiding spot inside a big round bale of hay which sat in the middle of a field full of such bales. Exhausted, she slept like a baby.

That night the sky was overcast, and Harriet could not see the North Star. She was slowed down by this, but not stopped. She felt her way along in the dark from tree to tree, feeling for the damp moss that grew only on the north side of the trunk and stumbling to the next tree. Though she moved at a snail's pace, she managed to keep in the right direction and keep moving.

Her next stop found her with a family of free blacks. For one entire week, they kept her with them, hiding her in a potato hole they had dug in their cabin floor. Harriet was grateful for having grown up on dirt floors—she liked the smell of the earth, and she felt no fear down there. When the way seemed clear again, the family sent Harriet on her way. She continued to travel by night and to sleep on the ground by day.

The next stop was a farm owned by German immigrants, people who became known as Pennsylvania Dutch. Harriet loved the tidy barns they'd painted black and the swept livestock corrals. Even the farm animals were clean! Harriet enjoyed listening to the Germans speak in their own language, too. They hid her in their attic until it was time to move on again, this time to the city of Philadelphia.

Harriet felt tremendous gratitude. It had been a dangerous and time-consuming journey, during which she had been the recipient of surprising hospitality from more strangers than she'd ever met face-to-face in her whole life—and most of them white! Not once had she had a sleeping seizure.

And now she was free! The thrill was indescribable. Not only had God seen her through, but He had shown her many godly people in the world who were willing to risk their own lives for her. In spite of being far from home and family, Harriet's heart was lightened by such knowledge.

Philadelphia was indeed a far cry from home. She'd never been in a city in her life, and Philadelphia was a big one. And cold! Harriet was a country woman, having grown up in a warm, humid land, listening to the soft sounds of birds and frogs and slave songs. Now she heard horses clopping on the hard streets and people shouting all day long. Instead of smelling the sweetness in the damp air back home, here she smelled horse droppings and frying food. It didn't feel much like the Promised Land.

But it would do just fine. Harriet was free. She made herself adjust to the tall buildings and the fast, noisy way of life. She got jobs working in hotels and kitchens. She worked two and three jobs at a time, partly for the money, partly to stay busy.

Because Harriet Tubman had a plan. Her escape had been successful. Since arriving in Philadelphia, she was meeting dozens of fugitive slaves, and she came to know the organizations that helped them upon their arrival. Harriet now realized that what a slave needed to get to freedom was courage, God's mercy, and the knowledge that it could be done. She wanted to help.

More importantly, Harriet wanted every one of her family members with her to breathe freely and walk where they wished and earn their own money, to live the amazing freedom she was living. If she could make it, they could, too! But they didn't know that, and they certainly didn't know how to go about it.

She decided to go back to Maryland as soon as she was able and spirit away her relatives. Maybe by now John Tubman would change his mind and come with her. Her heart leapt at the thought.

One day someone from the Underground Railroad mentioned that a free black man needed help to get his wife and two small children, who were slaves, north. The volunteers who helped fugitives in Philadelphia wanted a woman for the job, since one child was a baby. Harriet listened, then recognized the names of her sister Mary and her husband as the fugitives.

"They're about to be sold," the volunteers explained. "Your brother-in-law thinks they can escape, but Mary needs help with the little ones. Do you know of anyone?"

"Me," said Harriet. "I'll do it."

The volunteers were adamant that she not be the one. She was a fugitive from Maryland with a bounty price on her head. But Harriet laughed them off. "I'm not afraid. I understand how the Underground Railroad works, and I am the right person to bring them here."

And she was. So with the brave planning of her brother-in-law and a Quaker friend, in which the Quaker pretended to be a prospective slave buyer, Harriet's family was taken right off the slave auction block and hidden. They were able to escape to one "station," on to another "station," and then another.

Harriet waited for her family at a Quaker house in Baltimore. Then she confidently took them the dangerous rest of the way to Philadelphia without mishap.

Now with one sister and that sister's family free and with Harriet, she made plans to get more kin—and anyone else who truly wanted to be free. She knew now why God had taken away her fear. She knew without a doubt that she was to became a "conductor" for the Underground Railroad and devote her life to escorting slaves to freedom. That meant working and saving money for the journeys, staying close to the Fugitive Committee in Philadelphia, and eventually returning to the South.

Traveling back into the South to bring more slaves to freedom was just about the most dangerous thing Harriet could do. So many slaves were running north that in 1850 the United States Congress drafted and passed the shameful Fugitive Slave Law. Now slaveholders could track runaway slaves into Northern states, and those slaves must be returned if found. In essence, this law agreed with Southern slave owners that slaves were legal property of their masters and that such property should be returned. Furthermore, now it was a crime for anyone to help runaways even in the free soil of the North. The level of danger for a flight to freedom increased tremendously.

Harriet knew she was to be part of this mission of freedom no matter what the danger. She knew God was on her side. And God made Harriet fearless.

EIGHT

The Fugitive Slave Law of 1850, enacted one year after Harriet Tubman found freedom, was not a law made lightly. The fighting over it in Congress was long and wild. But in the end, the men of Congress agreed to it, hoping it would keep at bay the eventual war between the North and South that was even then threatening to break out.

Once passed, the new law was a perilous thing for a runaway slave seeking safety in the North, because he or she now might be returned to the plantations. And a returned slave was beaten harshly to teach him or her a lesson, then often immediately sold. Their lives, which had been difficult before their journey north, would be much worse from then on.

Not only was this upsetting to blacks walking free in the North, but whites who helped them were outraged. Now they could be arrested and fined for helping runaway slaves in their own free states. Since most of the sympathetic whites who helped runaways did so out of a sense of morality, they felt more anger than fear. They knew that, unlike their black brothers and sisters, they themselves would never be owned or whipped or sold.

They also knew this new law of the land was immoral and had nothing to do with the laws of God. So they felt no responsibility to obey it. Stories began cropping up of whole communities defying the new law and rescuing captured slaves before they could be sent south. A few man-hunters from the South were no match for a group of angry townspeople. Some slaves were spared in this way and sent on to Canada where there was no such thing as a Fugitive Slave Law.

Harriet began looking into the possibilities in Canada. In the meantime, she continued her rescue work. In early 1851 Harriet returned to her home county in Maryland to escort three slaves, one of them her brother, to Philadelphia. Then she went back again in the fall to the plantation where she had lived with John.

Of course Harriet had not seen or been in touch with her husband for two years. But she had dreamed of him constantly and truly believed he must miss her as much as she missed him. She was certain John would revel in her freedom and want to go north with her. Harriet, who was otherwise so sensible and keenly observant of the world around her, seemed not to be in the real world when it came to John. She was still deeply in love with her husband.

Dressed in men's clothing one night, Harriet found her way to the cabin she had shared with John and knocked on the door.

"Someone's knocking, John," a voice said from inside. The voice belonged to someone unmistakably female.

John Tubman opened the door looking as big and handsome as ever. Harriet stared up at him for a moment, speechless. Then she saw a beautiful young woman standing next to him. Harriet suddenly felt ugly and demeaned.

At first John didn't recognize Harriet in her men's clothes. He bent down and peered under her hat. "Harriet?" he said in a shocked voice. Then he began to laugh.

Harriet summoned a smile. "I came back to take you with me, John."

But John Tubman only laughed at her. The beautiful woman next to him began to laugh, too. Then John told Harriet that he'd taken this woman next to him as his wife.

Harriet shrank away from the doorway, speechless and humiliated, and John shut the door. She ran out of the quarters and into the woods where she sank to ground, full of wild emotions—love mixed with hate, sadness mixed with anger, awareness mixed with confusion.

Slowly Harriet realized that John had shown what he was made of back when she was with him and threatened to betray her to her master. Wouldn't a husband want to protect his wife? Why had she thought he would change while she was gone? And how could she have risked her life—her entire mission—to come to him? He was still a danger to her.

The worst thought of all for Harriet, though, was that part of her dream of freedom had included having her husband by her side. Now that dream was dead. John Tubman could not have been any clearer that he had no desire to be part of her freedom. He had taken another wife without even trying to find Harriet.

Harriet cried softly in the woods. Then she slipped to her knees and prayed. She knew the emptiness she was feeling inside would be with her for a long time. But for now, she had a mission. She was here in territory she knew. Surely there must be some slaves eager to go north.

There were. She gathered them that night, and together they made their way to Philadelphia.

With the effects of the Fugitive Slave Law making themselves seen, and with the death of the dream of married life with John, Harriet threw herself into her mission—to bring her relatives north and anyone else who wished to be free.

She continued to make trips to the South. She also found ways to guide slaves out of Maryland without going with them by drawing maps on their cabin's dirt floors and describing the stops for them to commit to memory. She would then personally escort the more difficult or complicated groups.

With this method, Harriet was able to help more slaves go north. Her instructions were so good and her routes so failsafe, nobody was ever caught, and she gained a solid reputation for successful escapes. People called her Moses. When a throaty voice from someone who could not be seen started singing a soft rendition of "Go Down, Moses" in the quarters, people knew Harriet Tubman was around and willing to help them escape that very night.

Or sometimes they heard a bird call and realized that it wasn't the season for such birds to call. Then they knew Moses was around. The next morning, several slaves would be missing.

Harriet had gotten very good at making the journey north. She knew the routes and the stations well, and her concentration was keen and her inner spirit alert to the suggestions of the Holy Spirit. This was especially important in times of pursuit. It was frightening for runaways to hear the sounds of bloodhounds and horses, but Harriet would softly sing, "Wade in the water, wade in the water, children. . ." to get the group into the river where their scent would be lost.

And sometimes, somehow, she just knew things she

could not know, and she'd find a way to keep her "passengers" safe. For example, on one journey north, for no apparent reason, Harriet simply sensed she and her fugitives were in more immediate danger. She put everyone on a southbound train to throw their pursuers off their trail; after all, who would expect runaway slaves to be heading south? It worked.

One time, to get to her former plantation to spirit away more slaves, she disguised herself as an old granny with a raggedy dress and a scarf draped over her head to keep the sun off. She bought several live chickens, which she carried, then she slouched down like a doddering old woman and hobbled down the road in broad daylight.

Of all people, who should ride up the road on his horse but her former master himself! Surely he would see the prominent scar on her face. Quickly, Harriet let go of the chickens so that they squawked and ran and half-flew every which way. Then waddling and bent over like an old woman, she chased after each one. The doctor watched for a while, chuckling as he rode on.

Sometimes the very thing she worried over happened: She would have a seizure and fall into a deep sleep while trying to run slaves out of danger. But during this sleep, the Lord sent her vivid dreams about what they should do and where they should go when she woke up. Harriet always obeyed these visions, even when they didn't seem to make sense.

While on the run, Harriet and her passengers slept by day and traveled by night. But one morning as they were settling down to rest in the forest, one of Harriet's dreams told them they had to keep moving all day, that the slavers were on their trail. She woke everyone up and got them going again. Then she passed out in plain sight in the middle of a road. When she woke up, her passengers were waiting for her out there on that road, the sun shining down on all of them. Harriet was horrified that they could have been seen.

But they hadn't been seen, and the Lord had given Harriet instructions in the dream. The bloodhounds were close—she'd been shown. She ran everyone back into the woods and zigzagged in every direction until they reached a river. Even though she didn't know this particular river, it had been in her dream. And in the dream, she'd been shown that it had a sandbar they could cross on.

The others were skeptical, but they had to trust Harriet. She started across the icy river, all five feet of her. Even though she waded up to her neck, the water never got deeper than that on the sandbar. Sure enough, they got to the other side. Eventually they found themselves on an island where Harriet ran them through the woods until they came upon a cabin.

Would the inhabitants be friend or foe? Not to worry—Harriet had seen this in her dream, too. She knocked on the door, and a family of free blacks answered. There the runaways were able to rest, eat, and dry their clothes by the fire.

The next day, they got back to the road via a different route and discovered by trampled grass, cigarette butts, and WANTED! posters that the law had tracked them down right to the very spot where Harriet had passed out. The bloodhounds had indeed been on their trail, but the zigzagging had confused them. Then the scent of the runaways had been washed away in the river, and the dogs could not find them.

Sometimes a slave was too frightened or too exhausted to go on. But Harriet made him go on, for the sake of many. If he turned back, the law would find ways to make him talk, and the entire Underground Railroad would be jeopardized. Slaves would be sent back to slaveholders, and white citizens would be thrown into prison.

For these reasons, Harriet always carried a gun. She prayed never to have to use it, but when a slave threatened to turn back, she aimed the gun straight at the slave and said with absolute conviction in her voice: "Go free or die." The slave never turned back.

In all her years as conductor for the Underground Railroad, Harriet never pulled the trigger of her gun.

NINE

As time went on, Harriet knew she needed to take her charges beyond Northern states and into Canada. Because of the Fugitive Slave Law and because Philadelphia was so often the stopping place for runaways, that city was no longer safe for free blacks.

Her first bunch of passengers to go to Canada started their journey just as winter hit. This trip took most of December to make, partly because this group numbered eleven, the most people Harriet had ever taken north at one time. And since they were going farther and during December weather, it was the longest time she spent with one group. It was not easy to keep such a large group moving, fed, rested, and cheered.

For some time the eleven fugitives hid with the great Frederick Douglass in cold and snowy Rochester, New York, near the Canadian border. Douglass was an escaped slave who was both educated and eloquent. He and Harriet had tremendous respect for one another's work, and he housed the eleven for as long as it took to get money and provisions for them to pass into Canada.

The town of St. Catharines in Ontario, Canada, became the destination of this party of eleven. There were many other ex-slaves living there, enjoying not only free lives but full lives. Harriet began taking all her groups to St. Catharines, one group every spring, one group every fall.

In 1854 Harriet began having unnerving dreams about three of her brothers back in Maryland. She dreamed they were being sold to the chain gang going south. She prayed for a way to get a message to them from the North that they must watch for her and come with her on her next journey.

Harriet remembered a free black man back home named Jacob who could read and write and who knew Harriet's brothers. Jacob's adopted son lived in the North and sent letters to his adoptive father from time to time, so Harriet asked a friend to pen a letter to Jacob under the adopted son's name. She couldn't use her own name, since she was wanted by the law in the South. And local postmasters would open the mail of freed blacks. If there was something considered dangerous or illegal in a letter, Jacob would get in trouble.

The letter was worded carefully. It read: ". . .tell my brothers to be always watching unto prayer, and when the good old ship of Zion comes along, to be ready to step on board." It was signed as if it were from Jacob's adopted son.

The postal authorities gave Jacob the letter and watched him read it. Jacob pretended to read it slowly and with much difficulty, though he'd read it quickly right away. Jacob knew his "son" had no brothers, and there were other clues that the letter was not from his son but nevertheless intended for Jacob to read. He memorized its words, then told the postal authorities that he didn't understand a word of it and handed it back to them.

Jacob had heard from a reliable source that Harriet's brothers were going to be sold with a lot of other slaves very soon. So he got to the brothers just as fast as he could to tell them Harriet would be coming for them.

Harriet arrived in December. She got her group together and scouted some provisions. Traveling north with her this time would be her brothers Benjamin, William Henry, and John. Also in this group were William Henry's fiancée, Jane Kane, who dressed in a boy's clothes, and two nonrelatives, Peter Jackson and John Chase.

When it was time to leave, Harriet's brother John Ross was not to be found. "I'll leave word how he can find us," Harriet told the others. "We don't wait." She left word with Jacob, then she took her group to the plantation where her parents lived.

They spent Christmas day hiding in the feed house near her parents' cabin where, blindfolded so that he could say he never "saw" his runaway children, Poppa Ross fortified them for the long journey ahead.

It was at the feed house where John Ross caught up with them, greatly agitated. He hadn't joined them earlier because his wife, Ann, had gone into labor. He wouldn't abandon her, and he ran for the midwife. Their child was born safely, and John had just left his wife and new baby, both of them crying. What made it tolerable for him was the knowledge that he would have been sold after Christmas anyway and the promise he made to his weeping wife that Harriet would come back for her next time.

This band of runaways made it safely north. And Harriet did go south again and bring back her sister-in-law, the baby, and another child of John and Ann's.

By 1857 all Harriet's relatives had made it north but her parents. And she'd been having disturbing dreams that those two old folks were about to be sold. Harriet knew they could not stand another parting if they were sold, this time possibly from each other. The time had come for action.

Harriet journeyed to the plantation where her folks lived and waited until dark to approach the cabin. The folks were thrilled to see her. Both of them moved so slowly from arthritis that Harriet knew they could not make this trip on foot.

Somehow she was able to find a horse and wagon. They loaded her mother's feather mattress on it, and off they went, traveling by night, sleeping in the wagon in the woods by day. Once they got out of Maryland and off the wagon, things got easier, and the trip to Canada was uneventful.

But Canadian weather was too extreme for the old folks. Harriet could see that they would not live long if she didn't provide a different home for them. So in spite of the Fugitive Slave Law, Harriet moved her parents into the state of New York. She correctly surmised that no bounty hunters would come that far looking for two elderly slaves who could hardly walk anymore. She bought them a house at 180 South Street in Auburn, New York, while she herself moved back to Canada. The winters in Auburn were rough, too, but they were milder than those in St. Catharines where Harriet lived and worked to pay the mortgage on her folks' house and to bring more slaves out of the South.

During these years, Harriet began speaking to groups about slavery and about her mission from God to help slaves go free. She relayed true stories of the Underground Railroad and was a compelling speaker with her deep and husky voice. The fact that she sometimes lay right down at the speaker podium and fell into deep sleep did nothing to deter folks from coming to hear the former slave speak. When she woke up, she'd simply pick up whatever sentence she'd been speaking before passing out. Harriet became a speaker much in demand.

In 1861 the Civil War began, the bloody war between the Northern and Southern states of America. At this point, Harriet Tubman shifted her efforts. She worked with the Union Army in a Confederate fort under Union control in South Carolina where she nursed sick, starving, and wounded slaves back to health with herbs and roots she gathered herself. She saved many lives in her role as nurse, and once again, her charges called her Moses.

She also worked with the Union Army as a scout and a spy. In 1863 she aided an army regiment of former slaves in raiding a Confederate encampment to rescue 750–800 slaves. They picked the slaves up in small boats and rowed them to huge gunboats while Harriet sang old familiar songs to them to keep them calm. This raid and Harriet's participation in it made front page news in Boston. The Bostonians loved this courageous woman!

She continued her hospital work for the army throughout the war. When the North claimed the victory, the ratification of the Thirteenth Amendment brought an end to the painful era of slavery in the United States.

After Harriet Tubman brought herself to freedom, she made a total of nineteen more trips back into the highly dangerous South. She was responsible for bringing out three hundred slaves that way, some escorted by her, some directed by her, but all of them brought face-to-face with the powerful and brave Moses woman who led man, woman, and child out of bondage with her courage and throaty songs. As conductor for the Underground Railroad, she never lost a passenger, and all arrived safely in the North.

During the Civil War raid, Harriet was responsible for rescuing another 750–800 slaves. Nobody knows how many lives of ex-slaves she saved by nursing them back to health in the camps through the war years.

After the war, Harriet returned to the house in Auburn, New York. There she worked to support her folks, and she continued her speaking engagements. In 1867 she learned that John Tubman had been murdered in Maryland. She never married again.

In total, Harriet Tubman brought well over a thousand slaves to liberty. Not only did she perform these tasks at great personal risk, but she let go of most earthly pleasures, comfort, and security for this mission.

In March of 1913, at the age of around ninety-three years, Harriet "Moses" Tubman died in Auburn, New York.

Mary McLeod
BETHUNE

ONE

Young Mary Jane McLeod stood next to her parents on the platform of the Mayesville train station and peered into the morning sun. It was October in Sumter County, South Carolina, but it was still hot and humid with not a hint of a breeze. The sun was a deep red ball hovering low over the tracks, indicating that another sizzling day lay ahead. But Mary Jane paid no attention to the weather. Today she was going on a trip for the first time in all her fourteen years.

The prospect of this trip was both thrilling and unnerving for Mary Jane, partly because she was taking it alone. It would be an eight-hour journey and would require that she change trains at one stop, something that sounded truly foreign to a country girl. But the most spectacular part about the trip was that this daughter of illiterate dirt farmers was actually leaving home—the very cabin she was born in—to live in the next state. This young woman who had picked corn and chopped cotton every summer since she was five years old and who had not been given the opportunity to read until she was eleven years old was going to Concord, North Carolina, to live with strangers. There she would attend a live-in school called Scotia Seminary for Negro Girls.

If she had realized that she would spend the next seven years away from home and that nothing in her life would ever be the same again, maybe Mary Jane would have been more apprehensive. But maybe not. Because this young black girl had a thirst for knowledge that could not be curbed, and even at her tender age, she knew what her destiny was. She was to learn all she could and then give back to the world whatever was given to her. In short, she was to get an education. And she could not get that in Mayesville, South Carolina. Not as a black girl. Not in 1889. So she was leaving home.

But Mary Jane was not running away. Her parents, Sam and Patsy McLeod, were strong, determined, hard-working farmers who had been freed from slavery a few years before Mary Jane was born, and today they stood next to her, stalwart and proud. Some of her sixteen brothers and sisters and their dozens of children stood with her as well. And as the morning sun began its slow climb up the eastern sky, the family heard others join them.

So proud was the black community of Mary Jane that they had taken precious time away from their work to come to the station and see her off. Dozens of farmers and cooks and housemaids and day laborers came from miles around and made their way down the dusty Sumter County roads in the morning haze. They came by mule, by oxcart, and on foot. Together they listened for the train's approaching whistle, and together they watched the huge steam engine approach. And when that grand piece of machinery stopped at the station with a mighty hiss, they watched with awe as young Mary Jane stepped up to it.

The black folk of Mayesville, South Carolina, had certainly all seen a train before. What they'd never seen before was a young black girl about to board one—much less all by herself. That's what filled them with awe. That's what made this such an event.

They joined the family and offered words of encouragement and handshakes all around. Some of these neighbors had helped Mary Jane's mother sew stockings and pinafore aprons for the young student. One of them had woven the basket Mary Jane carried on her arm. Some of them brought food for the journey. All of them offered their prayers for her success. Their belief that God had given this chance to one of their own was unflappable. They enjoyed wondering together about the strange, white Quaker woman clear out in a state called Colorado who had felt led to pay for Mary Jane's education. Well, after all, didn't God move in mysterious ways? Their very own Mary Jane, a brilliant, charming girl, was clearly on her way out of poverty and illiteracy.

Sam McLeod swung the small used trunk he had managed to acquire for his daughter's journey up onto the boarding steps. The neighbors shook hands with Mary Jane, and some of them wept openly. Patsy McLeod wrapped her arms around her sturdy daughter and said, "God bless my child!" Many in the crowd shouted, "Amen!"

Sam took his Mary Jane's hand and helped her up the train steps. There she turned to face the crowd. People called out blessings and promises to pray for her. Some handed up food wrapped in pieces of cloth—cold fried chicken, baking powder biscuits, fried apple pie. She tucked these into her handbasket.

Mary Jane locked eyes with her lovely, dark-skinned mother, a small, straight-backed woman directly descended from African royalty. Her mother beamed back at her. Mary Jane shifted her gaze to her father, a robust man of African and Indian descent, perspiring in the Southern humidity. He gazed back, the pride evident in his deep brown eyes. When the train began to make noises indicating it was going to roll, he called to her, "Get up in there, now."

Mary Jane moved inside the car and hurried to an open window where she could continue to watch her family members and neighbors smiling at her, nodding, calling out words of encouragement. Strange feelings ran through her. She had never been in such a situation in all her life, and nothing in her experience compared to it. She moved her hands over her coarse black braids, pinned up like a grown woman's, then down over her stiff dress made of a wool and cotton fabric blend, a dress sewn, starched, and ironed for her by her mother. It was good to touch these solid things, these textures, since everything else was feeling like a dream to her. *Lord God, stay with me,* she whispered inside.

The train began to roll, and Mary Jane's excitement began to surge—an excitement like she felt when she helped her sisters birth their babies. She could actually feel her heart beating. The neighbors waved and walked alongside the train, shouting over the noise of the engine as it slowly moved away. Then the train picked up speed until she could no longer see the station. Everyone was gone. All that was left was a humid wind gusting in her face.

Mary Jane stood at the window awhile longer. Already her surroundings were no longer familiar. She felt very little fear, however, though certainly she was a bit stunned. Rather, she was filled with exhilaration. Because Mary Jane McLeod —daughter of freed slaves, descendant of African royalty— was a blessed child in so many ways. She was loved, she was brilliant, and she seemed born with the gift of confidence.

The train went faster and faster, its steam puffing into the blue sky. The rhythmic clacking of the wheels on the tracks seemed to Mary Jane to be saying, *Scotia, Scotia, Scotia. . . .* She stumbled through the rocking car to a seat, sank down, and watched the piney woods of home fly by.

TWO

Mary McLeod was born in her family's cabin in 1875 in Mayesville, South Carolina, twelve years after the Emancipation Proclamation set American slaves free. She was the fifteenth of seventeen brothers and sisters, all given solid and expressive names: Sally, Satira, Samuel, Julia, Kissie, Kelly, Carrie, Beauregard, Cecelia, Rebecca, Magdalena, Hattie, Belle, William, Thomas, and, interestingly enough, Monday. At the time Mary Jane was born, many of her older brothers and sisters were already married with children of their own. In fact, several of her nieces and nephews had already been born before her!

This was a time in American history in which the recently freed black population was the brunt of violence and ill feelings, particularly throughout the South. Decades of slavery followed by resentment toward blacks because of the agonies of the Civil War left some whites very angry, and they made black folks their scapegoat. It was during those postwar years that the Ku Klux Klan was born, an organization of thugs who terrorized and murdered black people who had little hope for safety or justice—because, even though slavery was over, African-Americans had yet to receive their full rights as citizens.

Poverty for black people at this time was rampant. One African-American in later years would write that whenever there was a problem with the economy in the nation, the black people in her small Southern hometown were so poor they never saw a difference! Black Americans—particularly those in the South—lived an almost separate existence from white Americans.

In spite of all that, there was much happiness in the big McLeod family. For one thing, everyone was free, and that was a precious thing. Patsy and Sam McLeod had been born into slavery. They married as slaves and bore several children into slavery. When freedom finally came with the Emancipation Proclamation of 1863, Sam took the surname of his former owner. Now instead of being referred to as "McLeod's Sam"—signifying that McLeod owned him—Mary Jane's father named himself Sam McLeod. He and Patsy determined that their children would have a better life, and through thrift and hard work, they soon were able to purchase a small farm of about thirty-five acres and plant it with cotton, rice, and corn.

The McLeods didn't have much, but what they had, they owned. Sam built a three-room cabin on his own soil, and that was tremendously important to people who for most of their lives had not even owned the clothes on their backs. In the little wooden house there were a few pieces of furniture: a table, some benches, and a one-armed rocking chair for Mary Jane's grandma, Sophia. The floor was made of wood, which was far better than the dirt floors Patsy and Sam had grown up with. The family slept on straw pallets scattered about that floor. All cooking was done in a big stone fireplace.

Because of their deep faith, the McLeods owned a Bible,

a truly revered item, and it was prominently displayed on an open shelf. The fact that nobody in the house could read the Bible did not keep this family from loving it. It had been illegal for slaves to learn to read, so of course the McLeods could not read. But they hoped and trusted that one day someone in the family would be able to read that Bible.

Another reason there was happiness in the McLeod household was that this family loved the Lord. During slavery, worship among blacks had had to take place in secret, because plantation owners felt conflicted about slaves gathering together for church. On the one hand, some owners felt responsible for the souls of their slaves, and those owners actually provided Christian worship services. Others did not believe slaves had souls at all. They did not consider black people to be full human beings, and they treated them as such.

Still other slaveholders were simply fearful of any gathering of blacks lest those gatherings turn against the white man. Plantation owners gave slaves very little in the way of sustenance and no comforts whatsoever. Payment for backbreaking work came only in the way of basic necessities—a roof over one's head, some simple food, a blanket, the clothing on one's back. Punishment for any number of things was cruel—many slaveholders whipped slaves or broke up their families by selling individuals off to other plantations miles away.

These owners knew full well that their mistreatment of slaves could one day come back to haunt them—that is, one day, slaves might fight back. And slaveholders lived in terror of such a possibility. So group gatherings of any kind, including church services, were not allowed for slaves. Worship only took place in secret.

But since freedom had come, open worship was a way of life. The McLeods were praying people, and they loved getting together with their neighbors to worship out loud. They also loved to sing, and Grandma Sophia spent much time teaching her grandchildren songs that were called "spirituals." These were deep, soulful melodies that spoke to the spirit of the listener.

Little Mary Jane became a wonderful singer of spirituals, and she would sing them for the rest of her life, sometimes publicly. Their lyrics stuck by her, and she credited them for much of her strength in an essay she would write in her older years. There she would point out that, for example, when the spiritual said: "Nobody knows the trouble I've seen," it never ended on that down thought. It always ended with: "Glory, Hallelujah!"

Sam and Patsy McLeod lived as they felt Christians should live, and they taught their children to do the same. In addition, both parents were blessed with dispositions which greatly enhanced their demonstrations of faith— Sam was a gentle and kind family man, and Patsy possessed hope and determination against all odds. She taught her children that a combination of prayer and work would always get them by, and Mary Jane would take that belief to heart for the rest of her life.

So the importance of the Bible was two-fold. First of all, the McLeods knew it housed the Word of God, and that was a solid statement of the family's faith. Secondly, even though nobody in the house could read the Good Book, owning it symbolized ultimate freedom, because it had been illegal for slaves to read. In the recent past, slave owners believed that if slaves began to read, they might become enlightened in any number of ways, and this could mean rebellion against their white oppressors. Some black men had had their fingers cut off as punishment simply for owning a Bible. Sometimes the punishment was worse.

Now those days were over. Nevertheless, at the time

Mary Jane was born, blacks still lived without education, particularly in this part of rural South Carolina. As she grew older, she did not attend school for many years, and when she finally was able to attend a school nearby, it was open only four months out of the year.

So instead of putting her childhood time into school and study, Mary Jane, like the rest of the family, worked hard in the fields. The entire family—even old Grandma Sophia—picked corn and chopped cotton. The fact that these were the McLeods' own crops took some of the sense of drudgery out of it, of course, but it didn't make the work any easier.

Even the chores for daily living were hard in those days. With women having so many babies, there was always child care. Food for the table came exclusively from the farm—livestock and hunting provided the meat, and a garden provided everything else, including herbs for the only medicines the family would have. Consequently, living off the land and preparing its bounty for the table required extra work when the family members came in from the fields, no matter how tired they might have been. This meant they were toiling from sunup to sundown.

In addition, for extra money, Patsy took in laundry for white people, and she washed it in huge black pots of boiling water in the side yard. She hung the laundry on ropes strung from tree to tree, and sometimes she pressed the clothes with black cast irons she heated up in the fireplace. Then she and her children carried the clean laundry back to the white clients' houses in heavy wicker baskets.

Even though little Mary Jane was considered the favorite of her family, when it came to work, she was not pampered. From the time she was five years old, she labored in the fields like everybody else in the family. There were no laws requiring black children to go to school, and even if there were, for most of Mary Jane's childhood, there was no school available to black children in this backwater area.

So Mary Jane worked hard physically, and she became strong and disciplined because of it. By the time she was nine years old, she could pick 250 pounds of cotton a day. Just before she turned fourteen, when the family mule died suddenly, Mary Jane took its place, hooking herself to the mule's plow and pulling it through the fields on her own back to finish the planting. In later years, Mary would concede that these years of backbreaking work were hard ones, but she credited her upbringing for toughening her to hard work—any kind of work—and that would serve her well in the rest of her life.

Even though little Mary Jane worked alongside everyone else, the rest of the family saw her as special. Her mother claimed she was "born different" and that she always followed her own mind. She was considered a homely child, but she was bright and outgoing with a personality that would later be called magnetic. Even prior to formal schooling, her natural math skills were so superior that white farmers depended on her for accurate accounting at the cotton gin. Yet the lack of opportunity and the apparent lack of a way to get opportunity hurt her deeply. Day after day she worked bent over in the field and watched white children go to school. Day after day, she yearned to do the same.

One day when Mary Jane was ten years old, she accompanied her mother to a white family's home to deliver laundry. The family had two little girls who were playing with dolls and other toys in the yard, and Mary Jane was invited to play with them. They had a blue dollhouse with real glass windows, and she had never seen such a lovely thing. They also had pencils, slates, magazines, and—wonder of wonders—books.

When Mary Jane picked up a book, one of the girls said to her, "You can't read that—put that down and don't you touch that book with your black hands." This embarrassed little Mary Jane greatly. She laid the book back down and grew quiet. Years later she would remember that it "did something to my heart."

As she trudged home alongside her mother that day, she told her what had happened. Her mother listened. "Never mind, child, your time will come. You will learn some day."

"But when?" Mary Jane said.

Strong-willed Patsy McLeod clucked her tongue. "We will pray, child. The Lord will provide a way out of no way."

That way came a year or so later in the form of Miss Emma Jane Wilson, a young black teacher from the Scotia school who moved to Mayesville with a mission in mind. In 1886 she started a one-room schoolhouse for African-American children of the area called Trinity Presbyterian Mission School. At age eleven, Mary Jane walked the four or five miles to a one-room school every day and learned to read. She was so overready to read that she learned quickly.

Miss Wilson became a driving force in Mary Jane's young life. Her teaching went beyond the three Rs—she was a loving influence and a fine mentor. She recognized in Mary Jane a keen intelligence and superior leadership skills. She knew Mary Jane could—and must—get off the farm and share her gifts with the world. Miss Wilson determined that she would help that happen in any way she could.

By the end of Mary Jane's third year in school—which was actually altogether only twelve months, since each school year was only four months long—Miss Wilson had Mary Jane teaching newcomers to read right alongside her. And when a scholarship to attend Scotia Seminary became available from a benevolent white Quaker in Denver, Colorado, Miss Wilson made certain it was Mary Jane who received it.

It was nothing short of a miracle. Mary Jane McLeod had found her "way out of no way."

THREE

The year was 1895, and once again Mary McLeod (by now she had dropped the "Jane") boarded a train. This time she traveled to the city of Chicago, her first time north. She was leaving Scotia Seminary to be admitted to the Bible Institute for Home and Foreign Missions, an interdenominational missionary training school which would later be named Moody Bible Institute after the great evangelist Dwight L. Moody. Little Mary McLeod had a big dream. She felt led to go to Africa and be a missionary there.

After many years away from home, Mary had become more of a woman of the world, in a sense. She was more refined and knowledgeable about how to get along in every area of life than she had been back home in Mayesville. Scotia had nourished her thirst for knowledge and her curiosity about the world. It had turned her into a well-mannered young lady who knew she had a bright future ahead of her. Unlike many back home, no longer would her future include picking cotton.

Furthermore, Scotia had nurtured something in their

student that most black Americans did not have at the time—a daily acknowledgment of her God-given gifts, a plan for offering those talents to the world, and pride in her African-American heritage.

Mary's very appearance reflected that heritage. She had become a short, sturdy young woman with the strong African features which white America—and even much of black America—did not value: a dark complexion, full lips, wide nose, and textured black hair that resisted the restraints of white women's hairstyles. She would not be called pretty in any traditional sense, although someone once referred to her as a handsome young woman, a description which in those days carried plenty of dignity. And she was well-groomed, bright-eyed, and personable.

By now, Mary knew that her race, her gender, her rural South background, and even her strongly African features were all going to be obstacles in going forward with her dreams. But those were obstacles she planned simply to walk around—or charge through, if need be. She knew above all else that she was a beloved child of God, created in His image, and inferior to nobody. And there was great power in that knowledge. Later on, the novelist Charles Johnson would claim that she "treated racism like a puddle—she stepped around it." Indeed, even at this young age, Mary McLeod had dreams that would not be deferred.

Scotia had been the beginning of a new life for Mary. This was the place where Mary learned that there was a great big wonderful world out there and that she had much to offer it.

But the initial culture shock had been severe for a girl from a cabin in the middle of her daddy's cotton fields. Upon first arriving at Scotia, Mary was led into the school's brick building and up to the second floor. She'd never been in a brick building in her life, nor had she ever gone up a flight of stairs. That evening when she dined with the others, it was the first time she'd ever sat at a table with white people. She had not realized Scotia's faculty would be interracial. Seeing a knife and fork at her plate, she turned to the teacher next to her and said, "You'll have to show me, ma'am. Forks are just for white folks in Mayesville."

That night, for the first time in her life, Mary also used a toothbrush and slept in an actual bed. She soon studied Latin and Greek, mastered algebra, devoured great literature, trained in formal music, crafted fluid penmanship, and developed excellent debating skills.

She began the discipline of daily quiet time during which she read Scripture and prayed. In addition, she, like everyone else, participated in household chores at the school—laundry, mending, cleaning the kitchen. Scotia's policy was that students should know the practical skills of taking care of themselves, so the teachers and students themselves kept the school running in all ways.

The Presbyterian teachers at Scotia believed in what they called a "head-heart-hand" approach to education, and Miss Wilson had taught the same way back in Mayesville. In essence, this meant that a well-balanced education consisted of three parts: learning from books, developing a solid spiritual life, and mastering basic survival skills. Mary summed it up herself in these words in a letter: "Education—it's Greek and a toothbrush. Learning for the sake of learning, but learning for life's sake too."

During those years of boarding school, Mary McLeod had found her life's passion. Back home between school terms she had gone with her father and sister to a town ten miles from Mayesville to sell cotton. While there, they learned that the Methodist Church was having a speaker named Dr. Bowen.

Mary and her sister attended the lecture and listened to

the impassioned Dr. Bowen speak of the need for missionaries in Africa. Mary was smitten with the idea of going there and helping. She prayed that God would reveal to her the way she should go, and she came away from the lecture believing that Africa was her goal. She returned to Scotia with that dream lodged in her heart.

Eventually Mary McLeod had learned all she could at Scotia, and it was time to move on. Now she was an impressive young woman out to change the world, and to that end, she needed specific missions training. As the train huffed into the outskirts of Chicago, she breathed a prayer of thanks for such good fortune.

For the next two years, Mary studied at Moody. She then applied to the Presbyterian Mission Board in New York for an assignment in Africa. In a decision that caught Mary completely off guard, the mission board members refused to support an African-American missionary in Africa.

One can only speculate why a white mission board would decline a black missionary the opportunity to do mission work in a nation of black people. Certainly it spoke quietly of a kind of deep-seated racism. Most unnerving was that this policy was shared by most missions boards in several denominations, many of which rescinded the policy only in recent years.

The decision stunned Mary. She was used to the refusal of opportunity in the South among those who were blatant bigots as a way of life. It never occurred to her that an institution in the North—a Christian one, even—would have such views. She was gravely disappointed. She prepared to return home.

Mary McLeod Bethune would see many setbacks in the years to come. But the lost opportunity to minister to Africans would always be the hardest. It was to be the greatest disappointment of her life.

FOUR

Young Mary did not allow her setback from the mission board to affect her for long. She had inherited a strong will from her mother, and she considered self-pity a sin of indulgence. Besides, she believed that if this road wasn't open, God must have another path for her. So even though it would seem at first blush that her training to go to the mission fields had been in vain, Mary possessed a missionary zeal that could not be contained. She turned to the only thing available to an educated black woman at the time—she would become a teacher to black children, and she would embrace this new goal with all her heart and soul.

She returned to Mayesville to help Emma Wilson with the mission school there. During Mary's years away, the white community had apparently felt threatened by the prospect of so many newly educated children of black sharecroppers. There were fears that this new generation might not "know their place" and might become "uppity." Consequently, white authorities had reduced the school year from the original scant four months to a measly two months.

Miss Wilson had not yet arrived to start school, so Mary started it up herself—early. This was Mary's first real job teaching children, and it felt right. She would not be a missionary; she would be a teacher. Her vocation was in place, and she never looked back.

During this time in her hometown, Mary had the exciting privilege of teaching one of her older brothers to read, and it opened up a whole new world to him and the rest of the McLeod family. Since he lived in Mayesville, now there would always be someone nearby to read the Bible, the newspapers, and Mary's letters to their parents. Since Mary knew full well how the world opened up when one could read, she counted teaching one of her own family this skill as an especially thrilling accomplishment.

When Emma Wilson came back to Mayesville to teach, Mary moved on, looking for a teaching position elsewhere. She found one around Christmastime at the Haines Normal and Industrial Institute in Augusta, Georgia. This school was begun by a dynamic former slave by the name of Lucy Laney. Ten years before, Miss Laney started up with a few students and a rented cottage, and now her school had an attendance of over one hundred students taught by fifteen teachers. The school was by all standards a raving success.

Mary fully enjoyed her time at Haines, and she was a much loved teacher. She taught math, which was always her strongest subject. She also taught music and directed the choir. The singing students of Haines learned all the spirituals Mary had learned at the knee of Grandma Sophia, rocking in her one-armed rocker. These songs did not simply hold nostalgic appeal for Mary; they were also an art form from a suppressed heritage. What better way to teach African-American children about their ancestors and their struggle as a people throughout the years than to teach them the songs of American slaves? Mary was thrilled with the opportunity to pass these songs on to a younger generation.

In addition to teaching music students the value of spirituals, Mary came up with the idea of the Haines choir giving paid performances to the community. The spirituals were always a hit with the people of Augusta—both black and white—and the proceeds from these fundraising concerts helped the school pay for books and other supplies.

Because Mary was such a dynamo, spilling over with energy and ideas, she also during her time at Haines started the Mission Sabbath School for almost three hundred of the city's poorest black children. Her natural leadership qualities got a daily workout, and she became a much loved and popular figure in the town of Augusta.

After three years at Haines, Mary knew it was time to move on. She had learned much from teaching under Lucy Laney, and now it was time to take that knowledge to other places in America where no schools existed for black children. It became increasingly clear to Mary that her mission field was here, in the Deep South of the United States.

A plan began to form in Mary's mind. She would start her own school for black students, maybe all girls, using the techniques she'd learned to both teach and run the institution. She would have fundraisers and involve the community as much as she could. Above all, she would, as she would say, "Give as I got." That is, she would give back to the world what God had given her. This was always the motivation in this young woman.

While Mary knew a lot about starting and running schools, she also knew enough to know that she didn't know everything. Not yet anyway! There was more experience to be had before taking on such a huge project as opening a self-run school by herself.

She moved on to Sumter, South Carolina, to teach at the Kendall Institute. The same positive attitude and hard work she put into her previous job she brought to Kendall. And they loved her. But there was a new distraction at Kendall, something Mary had never contended with before. That distraction was a man.

It was in a choral society where Mary met Albertus Bethune. Ever the leader with unlimited energy, Mary had put together this choir herself in a local church. She was eventually drawn to the handsome man with the fine tenor voice.

Albertus was a Sumter native, born in 1870, making him five years older than Mary. He worked sometimes as a schoolteacher and sometimes as a porter. Soon enough, Albertus and Mary were smitten with one another, and they married in May 1898. Now Mary Jane McLeod was Mary McLeod Bethune. A year later, in February 1899, their only child was born, a son whom they named Albert.

Shortly after Albert's birth, Albertus was offered a teaching position at a school in Savannah, Georgia. So the family moved. There was also a position on the faculty available for Mary, so she was soon back in the classroom, doing what she was good at—teaching.

But the school was not impressive. It didn't have much of a library and offered little in the areas of science. There were no studies in African-American heritage, and the school did nothing to prepare black students in a practical sense for the world at large—a world which was, because of racism, lacking in opportunity and very often dangerous for these students because of their skin color. This, Mary felt, should not be swept under the rug but exposed so that black men and women could learn to deal with the ever-prevalent racism and yet still succeed in the world.

By now Mary had had extensive experience with good schools. She knew how they should be run, and she had a strong sense of what information and training were vital to black students. The "head-heart-hand" approach to education was the way to go. The dream to start her own school continued to build inside her. And her dissatisfaction with the school in Savannah fueled that dream even more.

There was another sense of dissatisfaction in Mary's life. She came from a big rambling family, of course, and family was much valued by her parents. Every one of their seventeen children was wanted and loved. Almost all of Mary's brothers and sisters had married young and had produced more households of children.

This had not happened to Mary. In fact, marrying in one's midtwenties was fairly late for a woman in her generation. Mary's independent spirit and her unique gifts and blessings had taken her in a different direction. She had already been considered a spinster when she married Albertus.

Perhaps years of self-sufficiency were what made her uncomfortable with marriage and motherhood. Mary herself was forever perplexed by the fact that she simply didn't take to either institution, though she certainly worked at it, just like she worked at everything else in her life. Whatever was behind it, for some reason her marriage wasn't working out.

Though Albertus was the reason the family had moved to Savannah, Mary became the reason they moved on to Florida, to take teaching positions at a mission school in the small town of Palatka near the Saint Johns River. In spite of their apparent lack of wedded bliss, Mary was committed to her marriage, and she seemed to be the driving force behind it. She also loved her son very much, though she never felt she was a very exceptional mother. In later years, looking back, she would confess that she found it more natural to look at her causes as her children.

In any event, at some point a few years into their marriage, Albertus left Mary and Albert and returned to South Carolina. The two never divorced, and Mary and her young son went on without Albertus, who died in 1918. Mary carried his name for the rest of her life, and there was never again another man for her.

FIVE

Mary McLeod Bethune stood on a knoll of white sand and gazed out over the Atlantic Ocean. Waves splashed along the barren Florida coastline, and seagulls dove in roller-coaster patterns, screeching with pleasure. After years of being inland, Mary found the shore and the salt air highly invigorating. She decided that it was near this shore in Daytona where she would build the school she had dreamed of starting for years.

At the beginning of the twentieth century, African-American workers from all over the South were pouring into Florida to seek employment building railroads along the miles and miles of coast. Tourism as an industry was only starting to raise its head in Florida, and the state needed tracks laid so that travelers could journey there by train. Most of the railroad yards were in the town of Daytona.

Most of the black railroad workers had children who picked up and moved with them. There were no schools available to these children in Florida, just as there probably had not been any for them in their previous state. Mary McLeod Bethune realized this, and she decided Daytona was the place to open her long-dreamed-about school. She would teach the children of these new black workers.

The need for education for black children in America's South at this time in history cannot be exaggerated. Church denominations often provided schools as mission work, much like Miss Wilson's school where Mary learned to read, but even those were hit and miss. Enough of these schools simply did not exist. Since laws did not protect black citizens, there were no public schools for black children and no truancy issues to enforce the schooling of black children. After all, who cared if black kids weren't in school? Not certain white authorities who felt threatened by educated African-Americans.

Mary Bethune cared. She knew firsthand the disadvantages of illiteracy and ignorance. And she knew that education for the children of railroad workers in Florida simply would not happen if someone didn't start somewhere. So she would be that someone. She would open her school, and it would emphasize all kinds of learning, from academic studies to vocational training for the kinds of jobs African-Americans could expect to get at the time.

She found a run-down shack which sat next to a garbage dump on Daytona Beach, decades before beachfront property would become worth millions of dollars. While of course working next door to a dump did not at first seem appealing, it turned out to be a blessing in disguise, because Mary knew how to achieve a lot with a little. The dump was treasure in which she found used lumber and all kinds of useful items which had been thrown away, and she was able to spruce up the shack in a variety of ways. She and young Albert moved in.

For operating expenses, she drew on her experience at working in all kinds of employment. She sold life insurance. She also baked sweet potato pies and yams, showed up at the railroad yards at lunchtime, and sold all that good home-cooked food to a bunch of hungry, homesick railroad workers.

Finally in October 1904, with, as she would claim in later years, "five little girls, a dollar and a half, and faith in God," the doors to Daytona Normal and Industrial Institute for Negro Girls opened—in the shack. Mary had no real operating expenses—she and Albert were already living very frugally. At the school, the students used pieces of charcoal for pencils and charred splinters of burned logs for a kind of fountain pen, which they filled with elderberry juice for ink. Their furniture consisted of wooden dry-goods boxes.

Mary's plan was to emphasize the three Rs ("readin', writin', and 'rithmetic") and an added R—religion. Her vision was to have another, as she called it, "dear old Scotia," in which she could teach girls both academic subjects and also vocational training in sewing and other domestic work. She would also work with them to help them see their value as children of God and to stay in communication with their Maker.

A unique long-term plan was for the school to acquire farm property so that she and the students would work the farm themselves. From that they could put food on the table and sell produce to support the school. In all ways, Mary wanted to teach self-sufficiency, right down to growing the very food that went into a student's stomach. In time, she hoped to offer more advanced education and nurses' training.

In the meantime, her philosophy of vocational training was broader than most. She wrote that it included "not only the technique of actual work, but intelligent comprehension of duties as a citizen and the ability to partake of the higher spiritual life of the world." So first of all, while white America may not have been ready for full citizenship of black people, Mary most certainly was. And she planned to make ready anyone in her sphere of influence so that when the time came—and she knew it would indeed come—that black Americans were fully recognized as citizens and even became civic leaders, they would already have superior skills and knowledge for the tasks at hand.

Secondly, Mary knew that life without a spiritual connection to one's Maker was no life at all. She proclaimed a personal relationship with God, and over the years she had developed strong personal faith habits—Bible study, prayer, involvement in her church. She would encourage her students to do the same.

She had also taken seriously the dictates of the New Testament to share her blessings. Mary Bethune owned very little. It is not an exaggeration to say that almost everything she ever acquired she gave away or used for the benefit of others. She always felt certain that she was on a mission dictated by God. In many ways, this teacher was a spiritual leader to her students and to many other citizens. And like her mother, she believed in the combination of prayer and work. Her strong ambition was directed and tempered by her love for her community. People saw it, and people were drawn to it.

Consequently, while Mary looked to the railroad yards for her students, she looked to the community for support, both in vision and from the pocketbook. Daytona had a population of only two thousand at the time. There were two black churches, and the pastors at both were highly pleased with Mary. They recognized in her a generous spirit, a brilliant mind, and driven energy, and they worked with her in any way they could.

At the same time, Mary had also learned over the years how to work with white people in a way few black leaders in those years had managed. The ever-resourceful teacher approached Daytona's new population of wealthy white tourists and appealed to their sense of generosity for funds for the school. It was successful. Not only did she receive much-needed money, but she developed an amazing inter-racial team by allowing white people to be on her advisory board. Decisions about the school were made by blacks and whites together. And in the South, no less!

One particularly prominent philanthropist who sup-ported Mary and her school was James N. Gamble, the wealthy soap manufacturer whose empire eventually be-came known as Proctor and Gamble. He agreed to become a trustee after listening to one of Mary's eloquent speeches about the needs of black children and the higher aims of education.

The specific need Mary shared with her audience at the time was the necessary addition to the school of a new brick hall that would house a chapel, a science lab, and a library. She waxed on about the lovely seaside location and the importance of her school to the community at large. James Gamble decided he wanted to see this amazing in-stitution of learning for himself, so he paid Mary's shack by the sea a visit.

Mary received Mr. Gamble as graciously as she could as he looked around from the shack to the dump to the ocean, then back to Mary. "Mrs. Bethune," he said, "where is the school of which you want me to be a trustee?"

Undeterred, Mary replied, "The school is in my mind, Mr. Gamble, in my spirit. I'm asking you to be trustee of a dream, trustee of the hope I have in my heart for my people."

Gamble was a smart man. He knew talent when he saw it, and he saw it in Mary Bethune. And he had not gotten his millions without taking risks. He was a fortunate man, and he knew it. So he decided to, as Mary would say, "give as he got" and risk on her dream. Amazingly, he invested in the shack next to the garbage dump and became a trustee in Mary's new school.

Gamble influenced other people of wealth in the area also to "give as they got" and invest in the dream. In particular, Thomas White, a Caucasian millionaire who made his fortune manufacturing sewing machines, contributed a great deal of money to build classroom buildings and even dormitories.

Mary Bethune's skill at reaching the masses of either race and infusing them with her own enthusiasm to the point where they would reach into their own pockets for money was something that would benefit organizations associated with her all of her life. Little Daytona had caught the vision. That was only the beginning.

SIX

Mary Bethune's school flourished. Indeed, how could it not? All her talents, her energy, and her missionary zeal were poured into this fledgling project. Consequently, Daytona Institute truly bore wings and took off. Within three years the school was able to move to a permanent campus in Daytona. A few years later, Mary purchased a farm nearby as part of the school. She had always wanted to teach students more than academic subjects, and now was her chance. Her childhood work experience on the farm was going to pay off, to the benefit of young girls who needed an education.

She taught the girls how to raise and harvest crops, both for the school's kitchen and for a brisk business in selling sugarcane, melons, pumpkins, tomatoes, and peas to the community. It became a familiar sight to residents of Daytona to see Mary and her students working in the fields before and after classroom hours in their school uniforms of blue dresses with white aprons.

By 1912 Mary's school operated with a full high school curriculum. The dream in the shack had taken root and grown in every possible way. And so had the lives of scores of African-American girls. Daytona Institute now had sixty boarding students plus a number of day students. It was one of only two high schools for African-Americans in the entire state of Florida. As more buildings and better facilities were added, Mary removed some lower grades in favor of higher ones, at this point even adding two years of college training to the curriculum.

But funding was always a challenge. The state did not support schools for African-Americans in those days, so to fund her school, Mary used every resource she could imagine. First of all, the students caught Mary's enthusiasm and contributed to the school's fundraising in a number of areas themselves. They sold the produce that they raised, cooked and served chicken dinners, hired themselves out as housekeepers, baked cookies to serve at afternoon teas held by wealthy white women, and sang in the school choir to a paying audience.

Mary herself worked nonstop at pursuing other avenues of funding. She had proven to be gifted at appealing to the generosity of wealthy donors. Often this was through personal contact with community leaders and even national ones. She was highly successful at her efforts, and word got around the country about this talented, ambitious woman who was educating black children in the South.

She managed to on occasion hobnob with philanthropists in the North, and she was able to raise money from them as well. But the truly unusual gift she had going for her was her ability to raise money from local philanthropists in Florida. The two gentlemen millionaires, Gamble and White, continued to help out. In addition, Florida's tourist industry had provided a substantial population of moneyed white folks with charitable leanings who were more than happy to donate to a struggling school for African-Americans.

How did the local whites know about this school? Of course Gamble and White helped spread the word, but Mary herself found a most creative way. She simply took her students to ritzy hotels in the area, marched them into the lobby, and started an impromptu concert right then and there. The Daytona Institute's choir would sing the folk songs and spirituals Mary grew up with—up-tempo melodies and soulful harmonies, voices sailing to the high ceilings of the ornate hotel lobbies. The performances were dramatic and engaging.

Then Mary—a superior orator—would take center stage to speak to the crowd about the importance of her school and its financial needs. She began by telling her own compelling life story, then moved on to her vision for the young minds of Daytona. Her request for patronage was always well received. She got the funds.

But it wasn't simply about getting money. Mary always had a burden for the community, and she taught her students to shoulder that burden with her and to do something constructive for their neighbors. Over the years, the school provided outreach programs to the community such as mission schools in the turpentine labor camps, summer school on campus for local children, and well-built playgrounds.

And there was community work that involved adults as well. Women received the right to vote in 1920, provided by the nineteenth amendment to the Constitution. But few people expected Southern black women to take advantage of it. Indeed, even black men hesitated to vote in parts of the South. It would be the late 1950s after much bloodshed in the Civil Rights Movement before Southern blacks would feel truly free to vote. But in spite of actual threats from the Ku Klux Klan, Mary and her staff voted in 1920. And they voted in every election after that one.

One of Mary's biggest causes was temperance. This movement to persuade Americans to abstain from drinking alcohol was prevalent all over the country at the time. Though today the serving and drinking of alcohol is subject to many laws and restrictions in the United States, that was not the case in the early years of the twentieth century. Enlightened people of the time—women in particular—saw alcohol as nothing short of evil. Too many men under the influence of alcohol drank away their paychecks or beat their wives and children or were the victims of senseless accidents.

Mary and her students joined the Temperance Movement. When this group from the Daytona Institute was able to influence the voters in a local election to keep their county dry—that is, alcohol free—it was clear that Mary McLeod Bethune was a community leader. Her influence extended beyond the classroom, and it extended beyond racial differences.

Mary's influence even extended beyond Daytona. She was receiving national attention from the African-American community. In fact, the national black press adored her. She was eloquent, passionate, and talented, and there was much praise extended her way for her contributions to improving conditions for the black community. Some journalists called her "the most glorious woman of the race."

With all the national attention of the time being bestowed on her, Mary had the privilege of connecting with Booker T. Washington, the famous inventor and founder of the highly successful and visible Tuskegee Institute. He came to the Daytona school for an overnight visit and was very impressed with what he saw there. This probably began Mary's lifelong habit of rubbing elbows with the famous.

By 1924 Daytona Institute was an impressive debt-free school. It had produced a large number of graduates, and many of them had gone on to be teachers in Florida's public schools. Mary was pleased with this. But she was not one to rest on her successes.

The student roster by then included a handful of males. Mary and her trustees had a vision for more male students, and they decided to make the school coeducational, for both genders. It looked like going coed could be better accomplished through a merger with another school. That school would be Cookman Institute of Jacksonville, Florida, a school whose students were African-American males.

This new consolidated institution where both male and female young African-Americans could attend high school and then go on to two years of college—still on Daytona Institute's campus—would now be named Bethune-Cookman College. Mr. Alfred Cookman himself was a white Methodist minister from New Jersey who had been passionately involved in social justice for black Americans. Now a black woman's name would be linked with a white man's name in an institution that would work not only for academic excellence and community service and Christian values but also for interracial commitment.

And its new president would be Mary McLeod Bethune. The little girl who had picked cotton since she was five years old and dreamed that some day she might learn to read had come a very long way.

SEVEN

The newly named Bethune-Cookman College was a huge challenge, but Mary Bethune had been getting ready for it all her forty-nine years. Now her vision of making a four-year senior college available to offer bachelor's degrees to African-American students was in full swing.

Fortunately, the merging of the two schools brought more funds onto campus. In spite of Mary's tireless and creative fundraising, there had been times when the money was not there for basic necessities, and at those times things were tense. At least once Mary had cut the heat off in dormitories when bills couldn't be paid. In 1933 she had suddenly canceled campus programs which had allowed students to work for their tuition, and a number of students had had to leave Daytona Institute. Those were dark days for the nation economically due to the Great Depression, and the school felt the effects.

Now thanks to the partnership, Bethune-Cookman College would have more stable funding. It was the only black college south of St. Augustine, Florida, and it was crucial that it stay up and running. Should it close its doors, many black students would not be able to get an education past the eighth grade. Now they could go through high school and on to an accredited junior college, which meant two years of higher education. And Mary's vision was going to take her school even beyond that.

She continued to be involved in the community at large and to lead students to do the same. To that end, Bethune-Cookman College provided adult education and opened the school library to the public. When Mary saw that Daytona's all-white hospitals were refusing to treat sick black people, she started a hospital for them at the school. She did much to bridge the gap between ordinary working people and the institution of education. They were all together in a journey out of a downtrodden existence.

The Bethune-Cookman College attracted national attention as it headed to four-year accreditation. Many celebrities from the African-American community made a journey to this exciting school. In 1929 the poet Langston Hughes was invited by Mary to give a reading at the college. It was an enjoyable time, and when Mary learned that he and a friend were driving back up to New York City afterward, she asked if she might ride along.

Mary had a knack for getting along with anybody, and Hughes and his friend were amazed at how easy it was to be in close quarters with the dignified and by-now famous college president. What amazed them the most, however, was how unusually easy the trip itself was. In those days, blacks traveling by car through the segregated South were subject to a lack of on-the-road comforts and even potential trouble in strange places. They could not be served in stores or restaurants, and there were no hotels available to them. Sometimes black churches would put people up for the night, but Langston Hughes, coming from New York City, didn't have those kinds of connections.

Mary Bethune did. The travelers lacked no creature comfort on this trip. Along the way, friends and acquaintances came to the rescue. As Hughes put it, "Colored people all along the eastern seaboard spread a feast whenever Mrs. Bethune passed their way. . . . Before Mrs. Bethune reached the wayside home of any friend anywhere, the chickens, sensing that she was coming, went flying off frantically seeking a safe hiding place. . . ." In other words, ladies in their kitchens along the route served up those hens in a tasty Southern fried chicken dinner in honor of their distinguished guest and her traveling companions.

A good story aside, however, segregation was surely not something to laugh at. Mary Bethune had felt its effects keenly since childhood. She treated it as a fact that needed to be dealt with, and then she charged on. Though she worked against bigotry all of her life, there were times when she utilized her skills at working behind the scenes quietly for the general good, and because of that, there would be critics who thought she was a little too friendly with white folks.

Much of Bethune's success, however, lay in her skilled use of language to communicate and acquire whatever was needed. When dealing with the civic matters, she was ahead of her time as she pushed interracial involvement. She could see that both black and white people needed to see members of the other race as their own brother or sister or at least as a fellow American with the same societal concerns.

She avoided using loaded words like "integration" and "equality." Those words set off strong emotions in white people, she discovered, and some black people as well. Rather, she used words like "democracy" and "patriotism," words that were universal to all Americans and distanced from racial differences.

But she was not anyone's fool. When a strange white man once referred to the matronly Mrs. Bethune as "auntie"—a term Southern whites used when referring to black women whether they knew them or not—she shot back with, "Now tell me, which of my sister's children are you, Jack or Joe?"

Another area in which she showed her strength and individuality was in speaking out about lynching. This practice of vigilante justice was perpetrated by some sadistic whites and ended in hanging black men from a tree. Unbelievably, lynching was an accepted practice that went unpunished right into the middle of the twentieth century.

A lynching meant that a gang of white men would "lynch"—abduct—a black man and murder him for any reason without any consequences whatsoever. Lynching hangings often were public ones. Sometimes entire towns would show up to watch.

The reality of lynchings remains an especially horrible and inexcusable part of American history. Though it was more prevalent in the South, lynchings also took place in the North. First Lady Eleanor Roosevelt attempted to influence her husband to pay attention to them and to enact laws or at least enforce existing laws to punish lynching gangs, whose members were often from the frightening Ku Klux Klan. But the president did nothing. Sadly, very few whites spoke out against lynchings, and blacks often feared reprisal if they themselves did.

But Mary McLeod Bethune, a Southern black woman, publicly took on the Florida governor in writing when two white men murdered a black taxi driver and were acquitted by an all-white Florida jury. She wrote to the governor: "What do you have to say about this cold-blooded murder? We appeal for your intervention and investigation. Is there no safety for any colored citizens in this state?" It was a brave thing to do in those racially turbulent times. The governor had nothing to say.

Eleanor Roosevelt did, though. She said, "I have real admiration for Mrs. Bethune and her devotion to her race as well as for her tact and wisdom." The first lady especially got to know Mary after 1936 when she accepted a government post and moved to Washington, D.C., for an appointment in one of President Franklin Roosevelt's New Deal organizations.

Among other things, Roosevelt's New Deal consisted partly of work projects the Roosevelt administration created to give a "new deal" in the form of government jobs to a nation impoverished and frightened by the economic crash of 1929 and the subsequent Great Depression. Roosevelt told Americans in his famous speech that they had "nothing to fear but fear itself," and then he got people back to work.

The National Youth Administration (NYA) was one of the many New Deal organizations established during the Great Depression to help young people get on their feet in a country full of unemployment and despair. Roosevelt personally called upon Mary to serve on its advisory board. She embraced this task with open arms. When the NYA continued into World War II, providing vocational training and placement for citizens into defense industries, Mary was made director of minority affairs in that organization.

She was considered a Roosevelt insider, meaning that the president himself listened to her suggestions, an enviable situation for any American. She had ready access to the president, making appointments with him several times per year in which she could discuss policy and plead her case for black citizens. Roosevelt himself often called her in for consultations.

Roosevelt enjoyed talking to Mary, considered her visits valuable, and saw her as a leading spokesperson for black America. Mutual admiration aside, it would be fair to say that the two of them saw in one another a useful person; that is, she needed social action, and he needed votes. They could help one another out in many ways, and they did.

Mary also had the ear of the first lady. In fact, Mary became friends with Eleanor Roosevelt and to some extent the president. But Eleanor's friendship with Mary was less formal, more warm and personal. The first lady was known for her compassion, and Mary sensitized her to black issues. White House aides watched Eleanor argue social causes with the president on many occasions, and sometimes those arguments had to do with causes for the African-American. Now both Eleanor and Mary appealed to the president on behalf of black America.

There was another genuine feature of Mary's and Eleanor's friendship. In Washington, D.C., a city very close to the Mason-Dixon line and therefore considered the South in many ways, Mary Bethune was routinely excluded from networking at women's functions because of her color. The color line was a solid one and hard to beat. Eleanor Roosevelt, however, invited Mary to absolutely everything. Those gestures did not go unnoticed by other Washington insiders.

In 1939 Mary became the director of the Division of Negro Affairs, a Civil Service Commission assignment. She was now the first African-American woman to head a federal office. It was a high position in the New Deal. *Notable Black American Women* would one day refer to Mary as "the most illustrious New Dealer" in the twentieth century. Indeed, she did see the New Deal as a dawning of a new era for black American citizens, and she let them know that on every occasion.

These were years of high national visibility for Mary Bethune. She was linked to virtually every African-American organization in the United States—was once even vice president of the National Associaion for the Advancement of Colored People—and she worked tirelessly with them and with government officials to gain wins, small and large, for black Americans. Every government agency that had anything to do with civil rights or government jobs knew they needed to work with Mary McLeod Bethune. This was not an unpleasant prospect, but she was a force to be reckoned with.

And yet Mary was much more than a Washington insider or bureaucrat. She chose her causes herself. In 1939, at the age of sixty-four, she marched on a picket line in Washington, D.C., with the New Negro Alliance to protest the refusal of a drugstore chain to hire a black clerk because of color. A marvelous black and white photo of this exists—in it the elegant and matronly Mary McLeod Bethune walks the picket line dressed in her starched dress, schoolteacher pumps, and Sunday hat.

She marched in another highly successful protest two years later that directly resulted in Franklin Roosevelt's most important civil rights action: Executive Order No. 8802, which called for hiring without regard to race in government and in defense industries. This was truly monumental. It established the Fair Employment Practices Commission, an organization instrumental in job-hiring fairness.

The work in Washington was exciting and valuable. Mary knew she was blooming where she was planted. She continued to work tirelessly at both her government post and her presidency at the college.

But for once, it appeared that her energy was limited. Working in two different areas of expertise located in two different states so far from each other in the days before fax machines and computers proved more than difficult. For the first time in her life, Mary had taken on more than she could handle. Her health began to suffer.

The college was also feeling the pangs of her divided attention. Mary took the first step at separating from the institution that had been her brainchild. She shifted her presidency at the college to a part-time post.

EIGHT

Patriotism was high on Mary's list of values. She had taught its importance to her students for years. Now she felt called by her country and in particular its black citizens to perform groundbreaking work in Washington. So for the present, she worked hard at both her government post and her part-time presidency at the college.

As the Second World War broke out, Mary Bethune saw clearly in Hitler and his minions the face of evil. Having grown up in the shadow of slavery and with the absence of many freedoms even as an American citizen, she was particularly sensitive to the horrors of fascism and Nazism. To that end, she wholeheartedly encouraged blacks to enlist in the military for the sake of freedom.

Back in Florida, Bethune-Cookman College had added a third year to its teacher education and had opened a new library. In 1942 it added a fourth year to the curriculum and officially became an accredited senior college, offering for the first time a bachelor of science degree in elementary education. Mary and her colleagues were thrilled. It had been a long, hard road to get there, but they'd done it. The NAACP was so impressed that it gave Mary its highest honor, the Spingarn Award. This was one of many awards she would receive in her lifetime.

But her health continued to fail. In December 1942 she made the painful decision to resign her presidency at the college. This decision was obviously a gut-wrenching one for a dedicated educator like Mary Bethune. But it was sweetened by the fact that during these World War II years, her work in Washington, D.C., took on even greater importance than it had before.

Now Mary's influence moved to the United States military. Even America's armed forces were subject to Jim Crow laws, meaning that they treated blacks and whites very differently, and such inequality was completely legal. Mary became special civilian assistant to the War Department, a groundbreaking assignment, working to break Jim Crow in the military.

In particular, while the formation of more women's branches of the military was an exciting new development, initially black women were to be excluded in the army divisions. Then Mary McLeod Bethune got involved. In a series of consultations with army leaders, she managed not only to change their minds about that, but she even persuaded them to allot a certain percentage of officer training to black women. This was unprecedented.

Never one to do only one thing when she could do several more, Mary took on another project in Washington, D.C., by organizing the National Council of Negro Women. In spite of her failing health, she poured her organizational skills and charisma into this new project and held the presidency there for fourteen years. It should not be surprising, knowing Mary's successes, that she took that organization to an amazing eight hundred thousand members.

Franklin Roosevelt died suddenly in office, and shortly after that, World War II ended. In 1944 Mary Bethune moved back to Florida, and she had one more task in her capacity as visible leader of black Americans. The world was changing after the horrific war years, and in a mood of global optimism, the United Nations was forming in 1945. Though the United Nations is now housed in New York City, it planned its first conference to be held in foggy, lovely San Francisco. Eleanor Roosevelt specifically requested Mary travel west to the City by the Bay for that charter gathering to help birth the United Nations. And she did!

Back in Florida, Mary had moved into a little cottage on Bethune-Cookman's campus and filled it with her many mementos of a fascinating life. Since she had retired from the college presidency, she now held the title of president emeritus. Her last organizational project was to form the Mary McLeod Bethune Foundation in her home as a place to house her papers and promote black educational advancement, interracial cooperation, and service to young people.

But her life was not yet over! One of the benefits of retirement for Mary was travel. With her job at the NYA, she had traveled cross-country several times, so she had seen much of the United States, and she had also managed to squeeze in some European travel. But Mary had a lifelong dream to go to Africa, ever since her youthful vision of doing missionary work there. In January 1952 she fulfilled that dream by traveling to the African nation of Liberia where she officially represented the United States at the inauguration of President William Tubman. It was as if things had come full circle for one African-American named Mary Bethune.

Back home, she continued to work on her foundation. She could be seen taking brisk walks around campus with one of her favorite mementos—a gold-headed cane that had belonged to Franklin Roosevelt and had been given to her by Eleanor, with whom she remained friends for the rest of her life.

Mary McLeod Bethune died from a heart attack May 18, 1955. She was almost eighty years old. The nation mourned.

She had been a woman to wear many hats—teacher, college founder and president, social activist, civic leader, patriot, even spiritual leader. The woman who was personal friends with First Lady Eleanor Roosevelt was often called America's Black First Lady. While she was alive, journalist Ida Tarbell had named her one of the "fifty greatest women in American history."

Mary McLeod Bethune was not only an eloquent speaker, she was a wonderful writer who penned and published several essays. Perhaps one of her best essays was called "Spiritual Autobiography" and was included in a collection of writings by well-known Americans about their faith. In the essay, this nondenominational Christian wrote: "There is in me always that deep awe and reverence for God, and His way of working in me. I feel Him working in and through me, and I have learned to give myself freely— unreservedly to the guidance of the inner voice in me." The power behind Mary McLeod Bethune's achievement was explained.

Sadly, the one hat that never quite fit Mary was motherhood. Neither she nor her son Albert ever felt good about their relationship, and he did not fare particularly well in life. Much to his mother's dismay, he dropped out of college. He then bounced around from job to job until he died in 1989.

Albert did marry and present his mother with what she considered her greatest blessing—her only grandchild, also named Albert. The pride of his grandma, this beloved grandson obtained his master's degree and found occupational satisfaction working as a librarian at Bethune-Cookman College.

Eulogies were written at the event of Mary McLeod Bethune's death. Columnist Louis E. Martin wrote: "It is difficult to understand. . .how much of a contribution a person who knew how to inspire others like Mrs. Bethune really made to the general welfare. She gave out faith and hope as if they were pills and she some sort of doctor." Poet and novelist Margaret Walker called her a "Great Amazon of God."

In her lifetime Mary McLeod Bethune received honors and awards too numerous to list. In addition, she was granted several honorary degrees from prestigious institutions including, among many others, Tuskegee, Wilberforce, and Howard.

She was the first black woman ever awarded an honorary degree from any Southern white college—in her case, Rollins. For Mary, that honor extended beyond the degree; it also meant that her driving goal toward races working together effectively and harmoniously was affirmed. The honorary degree was also a direct acknowledgment of her establishment of the Florida Inter-Collegiate Interracial Conferences for the study of mutual problems among black and white educators, begun and housed at Bethune-Cookman College.

As years went by after Bethune's death, scholars and activists recognized even more strongly the impact of her life. To that end, a statue of her likeness was commissioned, and in 1974 it was raised in a park in Washington, D.C., a short distance from the Capitol. It was the first statue in the District honoring either a woman or an African-American. Even in death, Mary McLeod Bethune continued to be "first."

Another honor came in 1985 when the United States Postal Service issued a stamp with her image as part of their Black Heritage collection. The picture on the stamp showed a square-faced, white-haired woman, her chin raised in dignity.

Mary McLeod Bethune not only worked at elevating the status of black Americans, she considered it vitally important to educate white Americans, as well—and she did exactly that, even with the president of the United States.

She was a woman any nation could be proud to call its own. Americans should pray to see her likes again.

Rosa
PARKS

ONE

It was early Thursday evening, December 1, 1955, and the downtown department stores in Montgomery, Alabama, were set up for their annual Christmas shopping season. Red and green holiday lights twinkled from storefronts at passersby who trudged in the winter twilight toward their destinations. Some of the Montgomery citizens flocking down the sidewalks in the waning sunlight were shoppers, some were workers headed home after their shifts.

Rosa Parks, a quiet African-American woman, age forty-two, was one of the workers. She'd been in a department store all day—Montgomery Fair, it was called—but she hadn't been shopping. Rosa worked there as an alterations tailor, and she was tired today from hunching over a sewing machine at the store making customized alterations. Her shoulder blades ached, and her eyes showed fatigue. But at least now she was on her way home, and that's all she had on her mind.

Like many African-Americans in Montgomery in the

1950s, Rosa did not own a car. The wages she received from altering clothes at the store and the extra cash she received doing sideline sewing work at home combined with her husband's wages as a barber simply did not support such an expense as a car. Unless a neighbor gave them a ride, both Rosa and her husband depended on bus transportation to get where they needed to go. Or else they walked. This was routine for most blacks and many whites in Montgomery in the mid-twentieth century.

But Rosa didn't like depending on the bus. She preferred to walk whenever she could, for one reason only. It was all about race.

There were strict rules in the South at this time that dictated most behavior according to the color of one's skin. These rules even extended to public transportation. Each city bus had a certain number of seats designated for white customers only—the first several rows—and a certain number of seats designated for black customers only—the back section. When black customers boarded a bus, they were expected to sit in the back of the bus, whether or not the front rows were filled. In fact, they were expected to board the bus and pay the same fare whites paid, then get back off the bus and board from a different door in back that only black customers used.

In the event that the bus was filling up, white customers had preferential seating on all seats on the bus. In other words, if a black passenger was sitting in the first row of the black passenger section but the white section was filled, that black passenger was expected to give up his or her seat for the next white passenger, no questions asked, and move to the back. This happened fairly frequently. It was not unusual, therefore, to see a full bus whose white customers were all seated and black customers all standing.

Or a bus with mostly black passengers, sitting and standing, and only a few white passengers, all of them seated, and a lot of empty "whites only" seats.

In addition to all those rules, blacks and whites did not share a row, even with an aisle between them. So if four black passengers were in a row and one white passenger needed one of their seats, all four black passengers surrendered their seats, thereby making the entire row available to one white passenger.

Those were the rules of living in the South of the United States in the mid-twentieth century, a legal system of separation of races known as segregation—or more commonly called "Jim Crow." It didn't matter what age or social standing or cultural advantages one had, because, in the final analysis, skin color was what mattered the most. African-Americans learned the rules of Jim Crow at a young age. They learned to obey them or get in trouble.

Twelve years before, a young Rosa Parks had once caused a fuss about the rules on the bus. Since sometimes more mean-spirited drivers would drive off after black passengers had paid and stepped off the bus, one day twelve years prior, Rosa chose to walk to the back without getting off the bus and reboarding through the back door. She was ordered to leave that bus by the white driver, James F. Blake, and she'd been quietly furious about it ever since. From that day on, she chose not to use bus transportation whenever possible, and she would never board a bus driven by Blake.

Rosa's quiet defiance extended to public drinking fountains, too, where Jim Crow rules also existed. Signs were posted over drinking fountains indicating whether they were for whites or for blacks, and this also infuriated Rosa. She would not drink from a segregated public drinking fountain. She would rather go thirsty.

Though as a rule, Rosa Parks preferred to walk rather than deal with Jim Crow on the bus, tonight, December 1, she was tired and eager to get home. So she stood in line at a bus stop and waited for the olive green Cleveland Avenue bus, hoping she would not have to stand in the aisle all the way to her home.

The bus pulled up. Rosa was a little distracted that day and didn't pay attention to the driver this time. Instead, she lined up with the other passengers and silently paid her ten-cent fare. Then she turned around and got back off the bus with the other black passengers, moved to the rear door, entered the bus again, and headed to the first row of the black passenger section. She sank down onto an aisle seat next to a black gentleman. Two black women took the seats across the aisle. Now the row's four seats were filled.

At the Empire Theatre stop, the bus was filling up. People quietly moved up and down the aisle, jockeying according to their race. Black people stayed in their section, of course, but now the white section had filled up. The next white passenger would be moving into the black section, which meant that the passengers in Rosa's row would have to get up and move.

Rosa tensed up. Here came a white male passenger, expecting to get a seat. The well-mannered Rosa noted that it was especially discourteous that he'd be expecting women to give him a seat, and that certainly was not gentlemanly.

Indeed, the women across the aisle got up and moved for the man. But that would not be enough, since blacks and whites not only did not sit next to each other but also did not sit across the aisle from each other. Nevertheless, Rosa remained seated.

The bus driver looked in his overhead mirror. "I'm going to need those seats, y'all," he called back. Rosa's heart sank when she saw that the driver was Blake, the man who had kicked her off a bus twelve years ago.

The black man next to Rosa stood. Rosa swung her legs aside and let him out, then she slid over to the window and looked outside. There stood Montgomery's Empire Theatre, its neon lights gaudy in twilight. She read its marquee advertising a new Western starring Ray Milland called *A Man Alone*.

Everything stopped on the bus, all movement, all conversation as passengers watched Rosa Parks defy the law this December day. The middle-aged seamstress and choir member did not surrender her seat to the white man. Instead, she sat.

Blake got up and made his way to Rosa's side. "Let me have that seat."

Still Rosa sat.

"Are you going to stand up?" he demanded.

Rosa looked up at him. "No."

"Then I'm going to have you arrested," Blake threatened.

"You may do that," Rosa responded. And she sat.

By now the entire bus was caught up in what was going on. The Cleveland Avenue bus passengers may have wanted to get home on this chilly day, but they were not going to miss this drama. White people were shocked. Black people were mesmerized that this unassuming woman was defying the system. They knew who she was, and they silently cheered her on, though nobody made a sound in her support.

Later the press would report that Rosa Parks was just a workingwoman who was too tired to get up. But Rosa herself would clarify that misconception every time. Yes, she was tired, but "the only tired I was, was tired of giving in." She'd simply had enough.

Blake made his way back up to the driver's seat. There

was company protocol on how to handle "agitators" on the bus, so Blake called his supervisor on his bus radio, per company rules.

"Did you warn her, Jim?" passengers heard his supervisor ask.

"I warned her."

"Then you do it, Jim," the supervisor snapped back. "You got to exercise your power and put her off, hear?"

Everyone heard. The police were called, and many passengers, both black and white, began to leave the bus, some of them quietly asking for transfers. But many more black passengers stayed to watch. They knew Rosa's character was impeccable, and she was strong as a rock. If these white men thought she was going to get hysterical and give in, they would be surprised. And while it seemed inconceivable that this good woman could go to jail, just how was this going to end?

Two police officers arrived and conferred with Blake outside the bus. Inside passengers remained quiet, whispering among themselves as they watched the three white men determine Rosa's fate.

The three men boarded the bus. One officer wanted to reason with Rosa so that perhaps they could simply fine her and move on. "Why didn't you stand up?" he asked her.

Rosa did not answer the question. Instead, she said to the policeman, "Why do you all push us around?"

"I don't know," drawled the officer, "but the law is the law, and you're under arrest."

Only then did Rosa Parks abandon her bus seat. She walked with the police off the bus, into a squad car, and on to jail.

One woman, whether she knew it or not, had just taken on the system of Jim Crow. She could have no idea the monumental movement that would be jump-started because of this one, quiet, dignified act of civil disobedience. She could have no idea that the entire nation—the entire world, really, black and many white—would get behind her. She could have no idea the impact this act would have on Jim Crow laws and that she would one day be termed the "mother of the modern-day Civil Rights Movement."

Rosa Parks simply went to jail that December evening, and the rest of Montgomery's black citizens went to work on her behalf—and on the behalf of all black people living under Jim Crow.

Or as folk singers would later croon, "When Momma Parks sat down, the whole world stood up."

TWO

Her name was Rosa Louise McCauley—named after her grandma Rose—and she was the first child of James and Leona McCauley. She was born on February 4, 1913, in the town of Tuskegee, Alabama. This town was home to the famous Tuskegee Institute, the school for African-American students founded by the brilliant scientist and educator Booker T. Washington.

Tuskegee was considered a fine place for blacks to live, much more self-governing and self-directed for African-Americans than other Southern towns, which was one reason Rosa's parents wanted to live there. Rosa's actual birth took place in a handsome little wood-frame house with a front porch trimmed in bric-a-brac.

From the very beginning, the importance of education and hard work was modeled for baby Rosa. Her mother was a schoolteacher, and her father worked in tandem with his brother building houses all over the South. Rosa's mother wanted to make a stable home for her daughter and for the son who would be born two years and seven months after Rosa's birth, but her husband was rarely home.

It was certainly true that to do the kind of fulfilling construction work he and his brother did, they needed to travel to find places to work and then stay away from home building these projects that took months to finish. But James McCauley, not much of a homebody, also actually liked living that way, on the road and away from home.

His wife did not like it, however. By the time Rosa's baby brother Sylvester was born, Leona McCauley had had enough of trying to run the house by herself, especially now that she had another newborn. She and her husband had many a fight about it. But James was not willing to find a local job and stay home.

Consequently, the two determined that they could not resolve their differences, and they separated. Rosa's father moved north after Sylvester's birth, and, except for coming back for a few days when Rosa was five, James made almost no effort to stay in touch with his children. Rosa did not see her father again until she was an adult.

The family of three now moved in with Rosa's maternal grandparents, who owned and farmed their own eighteen acres near a backwater town called Pine Level, just south of Montgomery, Alabama. They grew vegetables and a small orchard of fruit trees and walnut and pecan trees. They also owned chickens and a few cows.

Though there were no cultural advantages to living in the Pine Level area, its lush countryside was a nice enough place for a child to grow up in, playing in the soil, milking the cows, fetching eggs from the chickens, and fishing in the rivers with the old folks. Since sight was failing in both of her grandparents and they could not afford glasses, little Rosa baited their fishhooks for them. Many a fine meal was caught with such teamwork.

There was another advantage to living with the

grandparents. Rosa heard stories about her family lineage from these proud, freedom-loving old folks, the only black people in the area to own land. She learned that her great-grandmother Mary Jane Nobles, a black midwife with no white blood in her whatsoever, had been a slave, and her great-grandfather James Percival, a white man of Scottish and Irish descent, had been an indentured servant.

Slaves in America were almost always descended from black Africans who had been kidnapped from their homeland, enslaved, and brought to America to be bought and sold from before the American Revolution until the end of the Civil War. Indentured servants, however, were usually poor white Europeans who were working off a debt to someone. Sometimes they became debtors by placing their fate in the hands of a wealthy patron to get to America. They were then expected to pay off that debt by working only for that person for no pay for years, sometimes forever. An indentured servant had no rights granted other citizens. It was one step up from slavery.

Rosa barely remembered these two great-grandparents who met and managed to marry during the days of slavery when interracial marriages were illegal. Their first three children—including Grandma Rose—were born into slavery, and the next six children were born free. It would soon appear that Rosa had inherited some of their strong and defiant natures just as much as she had inherited their physical features.

Rosa also learned about her paternal side. She learned one great-grandfather was a white plantation owner and that her great-grandmother, a woman of both African and Native American heritage, was one of his slaves. Actually, three of Rosa's great-grandparents were white people, and consequently, all of Rosa's relatives—and Rosa herself—were light-skinned. Some of them were even mistaken for white on occasion.

Sometimes light skin tones could work favorably for black people when dealing with white people in the South. But Rosa's family did not take advantage of their complexions at all. In fact, they resisted most interaction with whites. They even discouraged young Rosa and Sylvester from playing with white children.

This had to do with survival more than feelings of racism. As a rule, in such a segregated society, black children and white children did not often interact, but they would on occasion. The old folks held no ill will toward white people, but they had learned relationships with them could not be trusted, and those difficulties started young. They did not want their grandchildren to be put in positions where they had to defer to white children, and that certainly would happen if they were playing together.

When Rosa was small, the Ku Klux Klan was very active in Pine Level. This was right after World War I, when black soldiers returned from overseas expecting to be treated like the war heroes they were. And that was simply not going to happen in the South. So the Ku Klux Klan kept busy terrorizing black veterans, thereby letting them know that they would still need to "stay in their place." Rosa's grandparents' farm was on a main road, and Klansmen would ride by on occasion, off to no good. This was a fearsome thing, yet little Rosa did not feel fear.

For one thing, her grandparents were not intimidated. Though Grandpa was a peace-loving man, he fiercely believed in protecting his own. Sometimes he sat up all night with a double-barreled shotgun by his side during these night ridings. He would not leave the house looking for trouble, but if trouble came inside, everyone in the family understood he intended to protect them. Rosa retained vivid memories of sleeping with her clothes on in case they had to leave the house in the middle of the night. Though these times were certainly unnerving, she did not feel unprotected.

Part of that feeling of protection came from the fact that Rosa grew up with a strong faith in God. Her personal relationship with Christ came early, and she was an active member of the African Methodist Episcopal (A.M.E.) Church her entire life, starting in childhood when she was baptized in Pine Level's A.M.E. Church. Founded by Bishop Richard Allen, this African-American denomination had a bold and vibrant history and counted as its members such illustrious personalities as Frederick Douglass, Harriet Tubman, and Sojourner Truth. In fact, the A.M.E. Church was called "The Freedom Church" during the days of the abolition movement, and it still stands as a strong denomination today.

In the rural South, most churches were not large enough to support a full-time pastor or really even a part-time one. Preachers rode "circuits," rotating between a few churches. Such was the case in Pine Level—the A.M.E. Church met every third Sunday of the month when the preacher was in town, and on the other Sundays, Rosa's family attended a Baptist church rather than miss a service. Rosa enjoyed church. She loved dressing up and meeting people and listening to the preaching. And she loved to sing in the choir.

The family faith was apparent at home, not just at church. Every day before supper and before services on Sundays, Rosa's family had devotions where the Bible would be read and Grandpa would pray. The family also had daily devotions even before going out to pick cotton in the field.

By watching her relatives, Rosa learned to turn to the Bible for guidance, and she grew to love its stories, wisdom, and comfort. Grandma Rose's eyesight being bad, she often asked little Rosa to read the Bible to her. Rosa would always credit those hours of reading aloud as one of the most important teachings in her life. Scripture became real and alive to her as a child.

In particular, the Old Testament spoke to her, especially the plight of the children of Israel. And she loved the Psalms, many of which spoke about fear. Her mother read the Psalms to her from the time Rosa was a tiny thing, and those Scriptures stuck with her throughout her life. One of her favorite passages is found in Psalm 27:1–7:

> *The LORD is my light and my salvation;*
> *whom shall I fear?*
> *The LORD is the strength of my life;*
> *of whom shall I be afraid?*
> *When the wicked, even mine enemies and my foes,*
> *came upon me to eat up my flesh, they stumbled and fell.*
> *Though an host should encamp against me,*
> *my heart shall not fear:*
> *Though war should rise against me,*
> *in this will I be confident.*
> *One thing have I desired of the LORD,*
> *that will I seek after;*
> *That I may dwell in the house of the LORD*
> *all the days of my life, to behold the beauty of the*
> *LORD, and to enquire in his temple.*
> *For in the time of trouble he shall hide me in his*
> *pavilion: in the secret of his tabernacle shall he*
> *hide me; he shall set me up upon a rock.*
> *And now shall mine head be lifted up*
> *above mine enemies round about me:*
> *Therefore will I offer in his tabernacle sacrifices of joy;*
> *I will sing, yea, I will sing praises unto the LORD.*
> *Hear, O LORD, when I cry with my voice.*

This psalm—and Rosa's memorizing of it—would serve her well in the turbulent years to come.

THREE

Rosa started school a year late. She was small for her age and chronically ill with recurring bouts of tonsillitis, so her mother held her back and taught her to read at home until she became strong enough to attend school.

But school was a disappointing experience for black students in Pine Level, Alabama. Though Rosa had exceptional teachers, school was open only a few months per year because of the farming calendar.

Rosa's grandparents owned their own farm, but most blacks in the area were sharecroppers, which meant that they worked someone else's land in exchange for a portion of the crops. In either event, farming required a rigid schedule of plowing, planting, and harvesting to which the whole family contributed.

Rosa's grandparents not only worked their own land, but at times they worked another white man's land for extra money. Rosa herself worked as a field hand alongside the adults from the age of six or seven, as did most black children, picking a couple pounds of cotton every day. Work in the cotton fields was hard and usually done barefoot. The pickers had an expression that went, "Didn't nobody have shoes on but the hoss and the boss," meaning that the only shoes in the field were on the overseer and the horse he rode.

Since black children needed to work alongside their parents in the fields for the family's basic survival, school attendance was not a high priority. The actual schoolhouse for black children was a shabby, one-room wooden building with some benches but no desks. The windows had shutters but no glass. A wood-burning stove stood in the middle of the room, and students and their families were expected to bring wood from home to keep it stoked.

White children, on the other hand, attended school in large modern buildings made of brick and built to last for decades. These buildings were full of shiny glass windows. There were desks and enough books for everyone.

Buses transported white students to their school, but there were no buses for black children, who walked miles to school, in all kinds of weather, and usually barefoot. Sometimes when the school buses of white children passed by Rosa and Sylvester on the road, white children would laugh and even throw garbage at them from the bus windows. This was very demoralizing to the young McCauley children, especially since Rosa felt protective toward little Sylvester. Righteous anger began to grow inside her.

One day when Rosa was ten years old, a white boy named Franklin picked a fight with her. When he tried to hit her, Rosa grabbed a brick and threatened him with it, though she did not throw it. Franklin backed away. Rosa went home and told her family what had happened, and her horrified grandmother began that day to indoctrinate Rosa on how to interact with white people, including white children. She ordered Rosa never to talk back to whites.

At first this was confusing for the child to be ordered by her proud and confident family not to stand up for herself. But her grandma Rose feared for Rosa's safety if she threatened whites with bodily harm. Rosa thought that she was right to talk back to Franklin, but she could see the anger in the old woman's eyes, so she stayed silent. Later she would realize that Grandma Rose was only trying to protect her.

This would not be the only run-in Rosa would have with white children, though fortunately she was never physically harmed. She often protected her brother from the taunts of white boys. What should have been simple mischief between children could easily have turned into a major racial issue. It often did with other children. But Rosa's sense of justice was outraged anytime she—or anyone else—was not treated in the considerate manner she would treat others. So she continued to stand up for herself and her brother.

Rosa's health improved considerably following an operation to remove her troublesome tonsils. She was able to attend grade school fairly regularly, but she was never particularly hearty. Eventually her mother pulled her out of school and taught her at home again.

As years went on, Rosa's grandfather died. Then her mother took ill. Then Grandma Rose took ill. By the time Rosa was eleven years old, she was carrying a great deal of responsibility, caring for the sick adults and her younger brother and the house. She also worked as a domestic outside the home for much-needed family income. Childhood was over for Rosa.

A few years later, she tried attending high school, but she needed to stop twice for family issues, to take care of her grandmother, who died when Rosa was sixteen, and her mother. Rosa would eventually get her high school diploma—a rare achievement among Southern blacks at the time—only after she married.

Throughout Rosa's teen years, she continued to take care of things at home—the farm, the sick relatives, her younger brother. In addition, both she and Sylvester worked outside the home for money. Rosa would later say: "I was not happy about dropping out of school either time, but it was my responsibility to help with my grandmother and later to take care of my mother. I did not complain; it was just something that had to be done."

In 1932, when Rosa turned nineteen, her life of work and responsibility changed. For one thing, she was about to become active in highly fulfilling civil rights work. And she was about to fall in love.

FOUR

In 1932 Rosa met a Montgomery man by the name of Raymond Parks. The two were introduced by a mutual friend and found they had much in common. He was immediately interested in Rosa, but she was not interested in him, at least not as a beau. So far unlucky in love, romance was not on Rosa's agenda.

She admitted in later years that she was initially not interested in Raymond Parks because he was so light-skinned that he looked white. If he wore a hat that covered his textured hair, he was even mistaken for white. Given the way she grew up, Rosa had an aversion to white men, and she almost let that stand in her way. So not attracted to Mr. Parks at first, she instead found a good friend in this handsome man, ten years her senior.

Raymond Parks—called "Parks" by everyone who knew him—worked as a barber in a black barbershop in downtown Montgomery. When he realized Rosa was not interested in him, he got her to pay attention to him by introducing himself to Rosa's mother, who liked him very much. She approved of his interest in her daughter, so one day Parks came to call on Rosa at her mother's house. Shy Rosa hid in her bedroom. She heard Parks politely say to her mother, "Well, if she's gone to bed, I won't stay," and he left without a fuss.

But he came back again and again. Eventually he got Rosa to go for rides with him in his car, a little red Nash. Owning a car was rare among black folks, and Parks was generous with the Nash—many times he piled any number of people in the backseat to give them rides.

Taking Rosa for drives in the Nash worked to Parks's advantage, because he was able to talk to her and get her to talk to him. Rosa soon discovered that Parks was an exceptionally nice person. He was a well-spoken, self-taught man with no formal education. They had much in common. Both had been home taught as children and had had to drop out of school later on, but both valued education. Both had taken care of older sick relatives. And both of them were very interested in civil rights work.

But Parks was more than just interested in civil rights work; he was risking his life and reputation already before the age of thirty in civil rights work. In his spare time, he was involved with the National Association for the Advancement of Colored People (NAACP), an integrated organization that worked to expose injustices toward black citizens. The organization had more presence than teeth in those years, but even then it was able to impact some concrete improvement in the lives of blacks. Parks's specific work in the NAACP was to find lawyers, mostly white, who could provide a fair trial for blacks in custody, not an easy thing to do anywhere in America at the time, especially in the South.

Among other things, Raymond was involved in what

became known as the Scottsboro Boys affair, a famous case in which nine teenage black males were wrongly accused of sexually assaulting two white women in 1931. The boys had been riding a freight train as hoboes. This was during the Great Depression when millions of people were out of work, and young men, black and white alike, bummed around the country on freight trains, going from town to town, looking for work.

An altercation between some whites and some blacks took place on one of these freight trains, and it escalated. The result was that a mob of angry white men waited at the next station for any black man who showed his face on this train.

Nine young black men who did not even know each other walked into this ambush. Forced off the train with sticks and guns and headed for a lynching, the boys were rescued by the local sheriff. He took them to jail in Scottsboro, Alabama, which of course was better than being hanged.

But the next day, two white women studied the nine teens in a line-up and claimed that six of them had raped them. The sheriff, in a stunning twist of logic, decided that if six of them were guilty, probably all nine were guilty, even though only six had been fingered. All nine were put on trial.

The Scottsboro Boys trial was full of travesties and famously lacking in any evidence. But since it had to do with black men doing violence against white women, these teenage boys were simply going to pay.

This kind of violence supposedly perpetrated by black men against white women was a common accusation in the South, intended to keep black men down. It was almost impossible to fight being accused in a system that routinely trampled over the rights of blacks. So nobody in the African-American community was surprised when the nine young men were found guilty and sentenced to be executed for this crime they did not commit. At the time Rosa met Parks, the Scottsboro Boys—the youngest of whom was only fourteen—were in jail and awaiting the electric chair.

Parks talked to Rosa at great length about the Scottsboro Boys. He was the first person ever to talk to her about this case, and she learned that he and other NAACP members were working diligently on the behalf of the nine young men by raising money for their legal fees to keep them out of the electric chair. They had formed an organization called the National Committee to Save the Scottsboro Boys, and Parks and its other members met in secret.

Parks chose not to tell Rosa too many details about the Scottsboro Boys organization for the sake of everyone's safety. He wouldn't even tell her the names of the others in the committee; he teased Rosa, saying that they were all named "Larry."

Joking aside, working for the Scottsboro Boys was a dangerous enterprise. Parks sometimes drove his Nash to Scottsboro and took food to the nine boys while they sat in jail, and even that was dangerous to do. The activists themselves could be killed for any involvement, but they were fearless and tireless believers in justice. And because of these selfless efforts, they were successful; the nine innocent young men were not put to death, though it would be almost twenty years later before they were all released from jail.

Such dedication to the cause of freedom impressed young Rosa. Parks was the first true activist she had ever met. She observed that, like her grandfather, Parks refused to be intimidated by white people. He was not meek; rather, he expected to be treated like the man he was. Rosa was impressed with his inner strength.

Before meeting Parks, Rosa had never really given voice to her feelings about racism, and she'd never discussed such issues with anyone outside her family. But Parks got her talking in the red Nash. They talked for hours at a time, sharing a similar sense of righteous indignation over society's racism as well as their feelings of hope for a better future. She began to feel proud of this young man who could be beaten or even killed for his work. And she began falling in love.

As for Parks, he was completely smitten by this bright young woman with the serene face, high cheekbones, and almond-shaped eyes that seemed to smile shyly at him from behind her eyeglasses. He moved quickly in persuading her to marry him. In fact, he formally asked Rosa's mother for permission to marry her, and in December of 1932, Rosa and Parks spoke their vows in her mother's living room in Pine Level. It was a quiet wedding, with only family and a few close friends present.

The young couple settled down on the east side of Montgomery and began an exceptionally happy marriage of love and mutual respect. These two people, possessed with tremendous character and integrity, held each other in very high regard. For the rest of her life, Rosa would sing Parks's praises at every opportunity. And he remained quietly supportive of everything Rosa did, insisting first of all that she get her high school diploma even though he did not have one himself.

One year after she married, Rosa received her diploma. Only one out of every seven African-Americans in Montgomery had such a degree at the time, and now Rosa was one of them.

FIVE

During the early years of their marriage, Parks continued to work as a barber, and Rosa worked at a number of jobs. She was at different times a seamstress, domestic, insurance salesperson, and office clerk, eventually landing the tailoring job at Montgomery Fair Department Store which paid seventy-five cents per hour. In their off time, Rosa and Parks enjoyed their church affiliation and poured their energies into the NAACP, the Montgomery Voters League, and other civil rights organizations.

It would be easy to think that life was mundane for the Parks family until the famous sit-down on 1955. But that was not at all the case. The Scottsboro case kept Parks busy working to fund the defense and attending strategy meetings at night. He and Rosa talked it through and decided that she should stay uninvolved in the Scottsboro case. Most civil rights groups that met in secret in those days consisted only of men because the work was life threatening, and Parks did not want to have to worry about Rosa's safety any more than he already did. He teased her that if they would be raided and have to run from a meeting at some point, he could run much faster than she, and she'd slow him down.

By mutual agreement, Parks also kept quiet about what was discussed in these meetings so that Rosa could honestly claim ignorance should she ever be taken into custody over Parks's involvement. Only once was Rosa ever involved in one of the secret night meetings for the Scottsboro Boys.

For some reason, usual meeting places did not work out this particular night, and the meeting had to be held in the Parks home. Rosa and Parks lived on Huffman Street in Montgomery in a small house, the kind of house which was commonly referred to as a "shotgun" house. This meant that every room led into the next room, so that theoretically a bullet could pass through the whole house without hitting a wall.

The half dozen activists met in the front room, crowded around a square card table. Rosa had known these were dangerous meetings, but it really hit home this night when firearms appeared on the table. The guns were protection should the meeting be raided by the authorities or the Ku Klux Klan. There were more guns on the table than men around it. Rosa had considered offering refreshments, but there would be no place to put them.

Seeing the pile of firearms set off alarms inside Rosa. She remembered all too well her childhood nights spent sleeping in her clothes while her grandfather sat with his shotgun guarding against a possible attack by the Ku Klux Klan. Now in her own home, she suddenly no longer felt safe. With the house being open from one room to the next, there was no place to get away from this frightening sight, so she slipped out the back door and sat on the back porch steps.

Rosa sat for a long time with her arms wrapped around her legs and her head down on her knees. Fear turned to depression. She began to wonder what the world was coming to when black men could not meet in a private home without fear of bodily harm. She sat there for a long time.

Eventually the meeting ended, and Parks came looking for his wife. He stepped out onto the porch, reached down, and lifted Rosa up from the steps. They went inside in silence. For years Rosa wondered every time Parks went to a night meeting if he would come home alive. Sometimes it was apparent that the police were watching their house, and Parks had to move about more furtively than usual.

After the Scottsboro Boys were spared execution, Parks and Rosa became more involved in voter registration through the Montgomery Voters League. Even though blacks could legally vote, there were complicated and racist rules surrounding their registration to vote that were meant to intimidate and prevent them from showing up at the polls. Parks and Rosa both learned to work with and around the system to get as many African-Americans as possible registered and voting, though Parks himself was never able to vote in Alabama.

Rosa's own work in the NAACP took shape during this time. She took notes at meetings. In addition, one of the functions of the organization was to document events in which blacks were victimized or discriminated against in particularly troublesome ways. Rosa heard many sad and horrible stories at the NAACP office, and her way of taking positive action became writing down those stories.

People called on Rosa and Parks at all hours to report things. Sometimes the people were terribly frightened, telling stories that they could never take to a white police force or even a white newspaper. Rosa's job was to stay calm and get the details down on paper, since the NAACP knew that the first step in finding justice was having these true stories in writing and on file. Sometimes the people whose stories Rosa documented went to prison or even were killed. Rosa often had to fight despair during these years and remind herself that a better time was coming. She relied on her faith greatly.

The late forties were especially bad for black citizens in the South. Once again, black veterans from the Second World War—including Rosa's brother, Sylvester—returned to their homeland expecting to be treated as well as they were treated in wartime Europe—and that was very good, indeed. In a knee-jerk reaction, violence against blacks escalated all over the South. Rosa would later write that "at times I felt overwhelmed by all the violence and hatred, but there was nothing to do but keep going."

In 1954 the United States Supreme Court ruled on a groundbreaking decision called *Brown v. Board of Education* which designated that "separate but equal" schools for children were unlawful. This meant that public school education, funded by government money, must be available to children regardless of race or skin color. Not to do so would be against the law. Simply put, racial segregation in public schools was now illegal.

Some people felt this was a sign that things would get better in the future—and they did to some extent—but for the most part, the hearts of Southern white Americans did not change. Now that schools were desegregated, many Southern whites, rather than give in to forced integration, ratcheted up the formation of private, whites-only schools, most of which remain in existence today, still catering only to white students. But thanks to the Supreme Court ruling, public education with all its advantages was now indeed available to all school-age children, regardless of color.

Rosa took hope in *Brown v. Board of Education*. The NAACP had been working for such a ruling since around 1925, and finally here was a success. Rosa believed that this historic ruling was a positive thing in the hearts and minds of most black Americans and that she would see an integrated America in her lifetime.

Now that segregation was illegal, the Supreme Court would be hearing arguments on how to go about desegregating the South. Arguments would be heard in the Supreme Court in 1955, but in the meantime, the NAACP was getting ready to suggest positive changes. Perhaps that sense of optimism is why Rosa accepted an opportunity to attend workshops on desegregation at Highlander Folk School in Monteagle, Tennessee, in 1955.

Highlander was an integrated (though mostly white) organization which had been offering training in the area of civil rights since 1910. It was instrumental in working with labor unions in the 1930s and in establishing more equitable teacher salaries for both blacks and whites in the 1940s, and it was often called "radical." Now in anticipation of putting the new Supreme Court ruling into effect in practical ways, Highlander was offering a ten-day workshop called "Racial Desegregation: Implementing the Supreme Court Decision."

Reluctant at first because of funds, Rosa consented to attend workshops there when a scholarship was made available and when some friends of the NAACP offered to pay her travel expenses. She wanted Parks to go, too, but he wasn't fond of travel. He was completely supportive of her attending Highlander, but he stayed home with Rosa's mother, who now lived with them.

Rosa traveled by train to Monteagle, where a white staff person picked her up and drove her to some handsome buildings that sat on a lovely mountain plateau next to a man-made lake. There for the next ten days Rosa made friends, most of them white.

The conference was very organized, much like being at summer camp. There were indeed several workshops on the nuts and bolts of desegregation, and there were fun activities, too, like square dancing and swimming. In addition to that, everyone had chores to do which were listed on a bulletin board each day. Rosa, who had taken time off her work as a domestic to attend Highlander, later wrote about this time: "One of my greatest pleasures there was enjoying the smell of bacon frying and coffee brewing and knowing that white folks were doing the preparing instead of me."

The workshop was one of many high points in Rosa's life of activism. She would later write: "I was forty-two years old, and it was one of the few times in my life up to that point when I did not feel any hostility from white people. . . . It was hard to leave, knowing what I was going back to."

The staff members at Highlander certainly were impressed with this woman's intelligence and quiet dignity, and over the years to come, many of them would write about meeting Rosa that year. They had known all along that they'd be hearing more about her in the future.

And of course they did. It was at the end of that same year that Rosa Parks sat in her seat on the Cleveland Avenue bus and refused to move.

SIX

After the police loaded Rosa into a squad car that Thursday evening in 1955, they drove her to the station. There she was photographed for a mug shot and fingerprinted like a common criminal. News photographs of her actual fingerprinting exist; in them, a serene-looking woman politely allows a police officer to press her fingers into ink, then press them onto paper.

She would later write, "Being arrested was one of the worst days of my life. . . . Since I have always been a strong believer in God, I knew that He was with me, and only He could get me through the next step." And the next step for Rosa that night was that she was put in a jail cell.

It took awhile to get permission to make a phone call, the right of any prisoner. Every time she asked for it, nobody would answer her. Finally she was allowed to make a call. She talked to both her mother and to Parks, who said he'd be there just as soon as he could. Then she was taken back to her cell where she waited quietly until Parks, by now quite used to working with the legal system, arrived with attorneys to bail his wife out of jail. The bail money was donated. Fortunately, Rosa did not have to spend the night in jail.

That night, however, Montgomery's black activists hummed with activity. A black college professor named Jo Ann Robinson had been trying for years to gather support for a bus boycott by Montgomery blacks. The humiliations of dealing with public transportation and its racism were many, and the bus companies simply did not care a whit about their black customers, their very bread and butter.

So far, however, Robinson and others had not been able to convince enough black customers that since they made up the majority of the riders in Montgomery, they could break the system by temporarily refusing to ride until conditions improved. Most black passengers had no other transportation, and without transportation, they could not work. A boycott was no lark. It would be a tremendous hardship on black citizens, and it would have to be worth it.

And what would make it worth it? A symbol. If one person could be used as a test case, perhaps people would rally. Many black individuals had run-ins with the system over seating, so plenty of debate had gone on over the years over who this one test person could be. Better a woman than a man because the press would be more sympathetic to a woman. And that woman would need to be above reproach. In addition, she would need not to have done anything wrong but refuse to give up her seat.

In the spring of 1955, many months before Rosa's sit-down, a teenage girl named Claudette Colvin had refused to give up her seat. In that situation, police literally dragged her from the bus and arrested her. Montgomery's black activists decided to use her situation as a means to get some changes. They took a petition to the bus company, not to integrate but simply to be treated better in specific ways. They also wanted black drivers to be hired.

The bus company took its time dealing with the petition, stalling rather than saying no. Activists began making plans to take Claudette's case to a federal court. The teenager was willing to go through with it, and she was getting geared up to speak around the area. Things were proceeding full speed ahead until it was discovered that she was about to become an unwed mother. This eliminated Claudette as a sympathetic person with the press. Disappointed Montgomery activists abandoned their plans.

But they remained ready and poised for someone else to take up the banner—so ready that when word got out even while Rosa was in jail that she had peacefully refused to give up her bus seat, Jo Ann Robinson took some activists to her office at Alabama State College at midnight and began making copies of a flier that had been mostly written months before. Rosa Parks would be the perfect symbol—a calm, hardworking, gracious woman of integrity and character, married to a solid citizen, caring for her elderly mother, with no bad behavior in her history and no police record. It was perfect.

Rosa had been in on earlier meetings herself when Claudette had proven to be a disappointment. She was fully aware that Montgomery's black activists were waiting for an appropriate person to take their case to federal courts. But she wasn't thinking about it that day she refused to give up her seat, as she later wrote: "I did not intend to get arrested. If I had been paying attention, I wouldn't even have gotten on that bus." She had already paid her fare by the time she saw who the driver was—the man who kicked her off twelve years before—and she simply wanted to get home.

In jail, Rosa had made the decision that she would never

again ride a segregated bus as long as she lived. So her personal boycott was in place. She had not yet caught on to the fact that she was the right person to take her case to court as a test case against segregated buses. It wasn't until she was asked twice by her attorney to be the test plaintiff that Rosa gave serious thought to allowing her case to go forward.

She talked at length about it with Parks and with her mother. They debated the pros and cons, and in the end, all three were in agreement. The cause of civil rights would be worth it, they decided. Rosa agreed to be the plaintiff.

Her attorney was beside himself with glee. Later he would tell reporters about Rosa, "I knew she'd stand on her feet. She was honest, she was clean, she had integrity. The press couldn't go out and dig up something she did last year or last month or five years ago. They couldn't hang nothing like that on Rosa Parks." Indeed, as Rosa put it, "The white people couldn't point to me and say that there was anything I had done to deserve such treatment except to be born black."

Jo Ann Robinson and the Women's Political Council made thirty-five thousand fliers to be distributed the day after Rosa's arrest. The fliers said:

THIS IS FOR MONDAY, DECEMBER 5, 1955

Another Negro woman has been arrested and thrown into jail because she refused to get up out of her seat on the bus and give it to a white person.

It is the second time since the Claudette Colvin case that a Negro woman has been arrested for the same thing. This has to be stopped.

Negroes have rights, too, for if Negroes did not ride the buses, they could not operate. Three-fourths of the riders are Negroes, yet we are arrested or have to stand over empty seats. If we do not do something to stop these arrests, they will continue. The next time it may be you, or your daughter, or mother.

This woman's case will come up on Monday. We are, therefore, asking every Negro to stay off the buses Monday in protest of the arrest and trial. Don't ride the buses to work, to town, to school, or anywhere on Monday.

You can afford to stay out of school for one day. If you work, take a cab or walk. But please, children and grown-ups, don't ride the bus at all on Monday. Please stay off all buses Monday.

The next day Rosa took a taxicab to work. Her supervisor was surprised to see her there, but she worked her shift.

A second flier was distributed later that day, again encouraging blacks not to ride the buses on Monday. In addition, this flier requested that people come to a meeting on Monday night at the Holt Street Baptist Church.

On Sunday churches all over town distributed the flier, and an advertising paper also ran a copy of it. As a result of this campaign, all eighteen black-owned cab companies in Montgomery offered to make stops at bus stops throughout Monday and charge passengers a dime apiece—bus fare—to ride in their cabs. This was a wonderful gesture. Nevertheless, commuting workers understood that those fleets of cars would be crowded, leaving no guarantee of a ride.

There was no guarantee of anything, really. Nobody knew if this boycott would even take hold. The community had never done such a thing before. And it didn't help that rain was in the forecast for Monday morning.

But, rain or not, the time had come for action by the

black citizens of Montgomery, and a collective fighting spirit took hold. Monday dawned and almost all African-Americans in Montgomery stayed off the buses. They took cabs, they carpooled, they walked. White passengers were so unnerved that they also avoided taking buses. The city buses were practically empty all day long.

That same day, Rosa did not go to work. Instead, she appeared in court, accompanied by Parks. She dressed simply and tastefully for her court appearance—a straight, long-sleeved black dress with a white collar and cuffs and a small black velvet hat with faux pearls across the top. Parks accompanied her through a thronging crowd outside the courthouse in which all the members of the NAACP were present. People shouted their support.

One NAACP member, a teenager named Mary Frances, had a high-pitched voice that carried over the noise. When she saw Rosa, the girl called out, "Oh, she's so sweet. They've messed with the wrong one now!" And she repeated it over and over: "They've messed with the wrong one now!" The rest of the crowd took up the chant.

The trial was a brief one. Rosa's attorneys entered a plea of "Not Guilty," but nobody was surprised when she was found guilty of breaking the law anyway. She was not allowed to testify on her behalf, but her attorneys did not fight that; the goal in taking a test case to a higher court required the verdict be a guilty one. Rosa was fined ten dollars plus a four-dollar court cost, which she never paid.

Later that night, Rosa and Parks joined others at Holt Street Baptist Church. But getting into the church itself was a wonderful challenge because it was surrounded for blocks around by throngs of excited African-Americans. Rosa and Parks worked their way through the crowd and into the church, which was packed inside with standing room only filled up, as well. When the service started, people stood outside listening through the open windows.

A new organization had been formed that day for the cause: The Montgomery Improvement Association (MIA). Montgomery ministers and activists had also made a decision as to who would be the leader of the MIA, and they had chosen a fairly unknown but impressive twenty-six-year-old Baptist minister named Martin Luther King Jr. Rosa did not know Dr. King, but she met him for the first time that night at Holt Baptist Church.

Martin Luther King Jr. was introduced to the crowd that Monday night, and he began by speaking glowingly of Rosa, whose good reputation had obviously gone before her. Of her arrest, King spoke the views most people were thinking by saying, "Since it had to happen, I'm happy it happened to a person like Rosa Parks, for nobody can doubt the boundless outreach of her integrity. Nobody can doubt the height of her character, nobody can doubt the depth of her Christian commitment."

He went on to deliver a stirring speech. He said: "There comes a time that people get tired. We are here this evening to say to those who have mistreated us so long that we are tired—tired of being segregated and humiliated; tired of being kicked about by the brutal feet of oppression. . . ."

Dr. King went on to challenge the crowd: "If you will protest courageously and yet with dignity and Christian love, when the history books are written in future generations the historians will pause and say, 'There lived a great people—a black people—who injected new meaning and dignity into the veins of civilization.' That is our challenge and our overwhelming responsibility."

The congregation cheered, applauded, and shouted, "Amen!"

Then the Reverend Ralph Abernathy read the list of demands the MIA would present to the bus company and Montgomery's civic leaders:

- Courteous treatment on the buses.
- First-come, first-served seating, with whites in front and blacks in back.
- Hiring of black drivers for the black bus routes.

The audience was asked to vote on these demands. They overwhelmingly approved them.

Then Reverend Abernathy asked the audience if they wanted to continue the boycott and to signify yes by standing.

Every single person inside the church stood. The crowd outside cheered.

A new movement was born. And so was a friendship between two quiet activists—Rosa Parks and Martin Luther King Jr.—that would last until the reverend's untimely death.

SEVEN

It would come as no surprise to anyone that the bus company would have nothing to do with the MIA's demands for better treatment. So the boycott continued. Every day, black citizens in Montgomery refused to ride a bus. They walked, they carpooled, they took cabs. And the boycott went on.

Eventually white housewives, who were absolutely not going to go without domestic help and could care less about what they considered local politics, defied their husbands and drove their black maids to and from work. Many a Montgomery African-American had a chuckle over that.

Documentary footage exists of this boycott, showing women in domestic uniforms walking en masse, teenagers piling in cars, white women chauffeuring their maids. The boycott continued for over a year—exactly 381 days—ending on December 21, 1956. It made news all over the world. The absence of black passengers—and many nervous white ones, as well—literally broke the system of bus segregation by financially breaking the bus companies.

The success of the Montgomery Bus Boycott is one of the most thrilling moments in the history of civil rights in America, and it kicked off many creative forms of civil disobedience in the South. In the meantime, the case went all the way to the Supreme Court, which ruled that bus segregation laws were indeed unconstitutional. At last, the demoralizing segregation on buses would end. Black passengers went back to riding buses, sitting anywhere they pleased.

The very first day, Rosa rode the bus. One of her drivers on that day was James P. Blake, the white driver who had twice kicked her off the bus. The press photographers had a field day snapping Rosa's picture riding on buses. Some of the pictures were staged for *Look* magazine, but Rosa was good-natured about it.

During the boycott, Rosa had lost her job. Eventually Parks lost his, as well. As the boycott year stretched on, both she and Parks found themselves virtually unemployable in Montgomery, quietly blacklisted from work opportunities, known as "troublemakers."

More importantly, life had become increasingly dangerous for Rosa and her family. All the community support in the world could not counter the harassment and threatening phone calls from angry whites. Even Parks, usually not intimidated, found himself unnerved at the many sick phone calls they received at the house.

Rosa's brother lived in Detroit, a place that had been very good to Sylvester. He feared for the safety of his mother, his sister, and her husband, and in 1957, with the help of a first cousin, Sylvester convinced his immediate family to move to "Dynamic Detroit" to be near him. The cousin sent money, and Rosa, Parks, and Rosa's mother made plans to relocate.

It was sad to leave Alabama. As difficult as things had been over the years, the Montgomery area was home and it was familiar. And none of them had ever lived in the kind of cold weather Michigan was known for.

Nevertheless, Rosa set about selling furniture and packing up their things for the move. Before they left, they were surprised by Montgomery activists who threw a farewell party for them, raising hundreds of dollars to help them out in their move north.

Rosa and her family lived quietly in Detroit, where Parks obtained his Michigan barber's license. Rosa enjoyed being near Sylvester and getting to know his thirteen children. She also became a deaconess in a small A.M.E. church.

At first Rosa did seamstress work in Detroit. Then in 1965 she took a job working in the office of Congressman John Conyers, an African-American attorney in Detroit whose slogan was, "Jobs, Justice, Peace." She first publicly endorsed Conyers's campaign, and she even persuaded Martin Luther King Jr. to endorse him. Conyers was tremendously flattered by the presence of such a notable civil rights figure in his campaign, and her approval of him was beneficial to him politically for years to come. When he asked her to work for him for pay, she agreed to it.

Rosa performed clerical duties in the Conyers office and also did more rewarding tasks such as finding housing for homeless people. Working for Conyers proved to be the perfect job for this brilliant yet previously underemployed woman. And he was thrilled to have her on his team.

In the years that followed, the Civil Rights Movement continued to make news and make ground. Segregation's back was broken time after time. Rosa traveled sometimes giving speeches for the movement, and she was part of the exciting March on Washington where Dr. King gave his famous "I Have a Dream" speech. Both there and back in Detroit, Rosa continued giving prayerful attention to the progress of civil rights for African-Americans.

Indeed, prayer was a very important thing in the movement. Most African-American freedom fighters were believers in Christ from childhood, and prayer was important to keep them from giving in to hate. The workers would depend on certain hymns to keep them going, many of the songs spirituals from the days of slavery.

When civil rights workers sang such songs, they knew—like the children of Israel knew—that there would be no turning back in this fight for freedom, no matter what the dangers were. And these days, Rosa noted, danger was everywhere and more open. Bombings, lynchings, shootings, beatings, rioting—the decades of the fifties and sixties were volatile times in American race relations.

In the spring of 1968, a deranged woman stabbed Dr. Martin Luther King in New York. Though his injury was only minor, Rosa felt increasingly uneasy at how dangerous things were for her dear friend.

Ten days later, Dr. King was assassinated by a lone gunman while standing on the balcony of his motel in Memphis, Tennessee. Rosa and her mother were listening to a minister on the radio when the broadcast was interrupted by the horrible news. Stunned, she and her mother wrapped their arms around one another and wept.

On the day of King's funeral, Rosa found herself unable to stop crying. She recited the twenty-seventh psalm aloud, over and over for comfort.

Dr. King's death would mark the end of an era.

EIGHT

The 1970s were personally difficult years for Rosa in that every member of her small family contracted cancer. At one point, she was running between three different hospitals, and then, sadly, everyone died in a three-year span. Her beloved Parks died in 1977, and her baby brother, Sylvester, followed a few months later. Two years later her mother died.

Rosa was now alone in Detroit. The loss of her husband, in particular, created a vast void in her life as they were very devoted to one another. They had never had children, and these threatened to be lonely years for this woman, who was also aging. But Rosa drew on her faith and took comfort in knowing that all three of her loved ones were in a better place and that she would be reunited with them one day.

Rosa stayed in Detroit, a city so proud that this famous civil rights worker had chosen to live there that it renamed one of its streets Rosa Parks Boulevard. Rosa remained active in the NAACP.

In 1987 she cofounded—with her good friend Elaine

Steele—the Rosa and Raymond Parks Institute for Self-Development in Detroit. The purpose for this organization was to motivate and direct youth in achieving their highest potential. Rosa especially wanted her husband's name on this foundation because he was a worker for African-American freedoms long before the Supreme Court ever got involved with such freedoms. The Rosa and Raymond Parks Institute for Self-Development would offer education for youth in the areas of communication, economic skills, politics, and health awareness. In addition, the institute would provide scholarships for motivated young people.

The following year, Rosa retired from twenty-three years of working for Congressman John Conyers. She had loved being involved over the years in political work in such a vibrant place as Detroit and with a congressman she considered a mover and shaker. And her reputation had been good for the congressman's office. Conyers spoke glowingly of Rosa, stating publicly, "She's a living gem!"

The accolades continued. In 1990 the Kennedy Center in Washington, D.C., celebrated her seventy-seventh birthday with three thousand black leaders, entertainers, and government dignitaries in attendance. It was a gala event, and Rosa took the stage to speak on behalf of freedom. "Pray and work," she said, "for the freedom of Nelson Mandela and all of our sisters and brothers in South Africa."

As she neared her eightieth year, Rosa's work was not even close to being finished. She put her energies into promoting her new foundation. She also began a writing career. Before her famous sit-down years ago, part of Rosa's behind-the-scenes civil rights work with her husband had been the writing of those true stories of black people suffering indignities. It was valuable work that gave an ear to traumatized individuals as well as information to the world at large.

Now Rosa focused her documenting skills on writing

her own story. In 1992 Dial Books published *Rosa Parks: My Story,* an autobiography written by Rosa with help from a writer named Jim Haskins. Raised as she was to love books and education, publication was truly exciting for Rosa.

Civil rights leaders were pleased, too, now that the story of this American heroine would be told in her own words, documented for generations to come. Coretta Scott King endorsed the book, stating, "For a long time there has been a need for such books that illuminate the civil rights struggle. In these pages, Mrs. Parks has movingly evoked the experiences and influences that shaped her formative years, the events that led to her appointment with history, and her unrelenting faith."

Out of this book came a condensed volume for very young children called *I Am Rosa Parks.* This small illustrated children's book captured the many highlights of Rosa's life both personally and politically with four chapters titled: "I Get Arrested," "How I Grew Up," "We Stay Off the Buses," and "Since the Boycott." Now even small children could read about one of America's finest citizens in her very own words.

In 1994, in time to celebrate forty years since Rosa first refused to give up her seat on the bus in Montgomery in 1955, Zondervan Publishers published a book of collected essays and personal stories by Rosa with help from Detroit attorney Gregory J. Reed. The handsome book, complete with historic black-and-white photos, was called *Quiet Strength,* subtitled *The Faith, the Hope, and the Heart of a Woman Who Changed a Nation.* This book rounded out the writing by Rosa available to the public by including a great deal more about her faith and Scriptures that were her personal favorites.

But Rosa was up to more than only writing books during this late decade in her life. She continued to travel from Detroit to lecture and receive awards from around the nation and even the world. One of her favorite themes in her speaking was the promise of American youth. She wrote in *Quiet Strength:* "What message would I have for young people today—of any race? Work hard, do not be discouraged, and in everything you do, try to make our country—and the world—a better place for us all." Rosa respected the energy of youth and encouraged every young person she met. Young people, in turn, loved to be in the presence of this wise and dignified woman who thought so highly of them.

In 1991 the Smithsonian Institution in Washington, D.C., unveiled a bust of Rosa Parks, a tremendous honor for any American citizen. In 1994 she traveled to Japan to receive an honorary degree from Soka University. That same year she traveled to Stockholm, Sweden, to light the Peace Candle there and to receive the Rosa Parks Peace Prize.

But she made headlines in another, more unnerving way that year. On the evening of August 31, 1994, Rosa was in her bedroom in her house in Detroit when she heard a loud noise outdoors. She went downstairs to investigate, and right in her living room stood a young man she did not know. He was very drunk.

"Someone knocked down your door," the stranger said. Rosa said nothing and watched him carefully. Clearly he had knocked the door down himself. "I chased the guy away," the man claimed. "I'm here to protect you, but I need three dollars."

Rosa was not fearful. She went back up the stairs and fetched the money. When she turned, she saw the man had followed her up the stairs. She tried to hand him the money.

He suddenly became agitated. "I need more than that," he said. Then he began to push Rosa and strike her in the face. Rosa had never been hit like this in her life, but she quickly got over her surprise, grabbed the man's shirt, and fought back—even at the age of eighty-one.

The man began to shout. "You're going to make me hurt you if you don't give me all your money!" Rosa screamed for help, but since she lived alone, nobody heard her. She prayed for protection as she got herself away from the man's flying hands and quickly shoved all the money she had at him—$103. He grabbed the cash and ran down the stairs and out the door.

Shaken, Rosa called the police. She went to the hospital for treatment, but she was more or less all right. The press got wind of the story, and the entire world learned that a common criminal had roughed up the aging Mrs. Parks right in her own home. And the world was outraged. The black community was particularly incensed that the young man was African-American.

But Rosa was only saddened. She later wrote, "I pray for this young man and the conditions in our country that have made him this way. I urge people not to read too much into the attack. I regret that some people, regardless of race, are in such a mental state that they would want to harm an older person. . . . Despite the violence and crime in our society, we should not let fear overwhelm us."

Rosa remained hale and hearty after the attack, and she lived to help usher in the new millennium. In August 2002 she received the Walter P. Reuther Humanitarian Award from Wayne State University's College of Urban, Labor, and Metropolitan Affairs in Detroit, a city whose citizens continue to view her as their personal treasure.

As of this writing, Rosa Parks, the woman whom Coretta Scott King called "one of America's greatest freedom fighters," continues to live in Detroit. "I want to be remembered," Rosa wrote in *Quiet Strength,* "as a person who stood up to injustice, who wanted a better world for young people; and most of all, I want to be remembered as a person who wanted to be free and wanted others to be free."

FOR FURTHER READING

Brinkley, Douglas. *Rosa Parks.* New York: Viking Penguin, 2000.

Glazer, Tom. *Songs of Peace, Freedom & Protest.* Greenwich, Conn.: Fawcett Publications, 1972.

Lincoln, C. Eric and Lawrence H. Mamiya. *The Black Church in the African-American Experience.* Durham, N.C.: Duke University Press, 1990.

McCluskey, Audrey Thomas and Elaine M. Smith. *Mary McLeod Bethune.* Bloomington: Indiana University Press, 1999.

Parks, Rosa, with Jim Haskins. *I Am Rosa Parks.* New York: Penguin Putnam, 1997.

Parks, Rosa, with Jim Haskins. *My Story.* New York: Dial Books, 1992.

Parks, Rosa, with Gregory Reed. *Quiet Strength.* Grand Rapids, Mich.: Zondervan Publishing House, 1994.

Pennington, James W. C. *The Fugitive Blacksmith.* London: Charles Gilpin Company, 1849.

Petry, Ann. *Harriet Tubman.* New York: Thomas Y. Crowell Company, 1955.

Rice, C. Duncan. *The Rise and Fall of Black Slavery.* Baton Rouge: Louisiana State University Press, 1975.

Still, William. *The Underground Railroad.* Chicago: Johnson Publishing Company, 1970.

Young, Andrew. *A Way Out of No Way: The Spiritual Memoirs of Andrew Young.* Nashville: Thomas Nelson, 1994.